EVALUATING YOUR AGENCY'S PROGRAMS

SAGE HUMAN SERVICES GUIDES, VOLUME 29

Barbara Selade

SAGE HUMAN SERVICES GUIDES

a series of books edited by ARMAND LAUFFER and published in cooperation with the University of Michigan School of Social Work.

A **SAGE** HUMAN SERVICES GUIDE **29**

EVALUATING YOUR AGENCY'S PROGRAMS

Michael J. AUSTIN, Gary COX, Naomi GOTTLIEB,
J. David HAWKINS, Jean M. KRUZICH,
and Ronald RAUCH

*Published in cooperation with the Center for Social Welfare Research of the
University of Washington School of Social Work, and the continuing
Education Program in the Human Services of the University of Michigan
School of Social Work*

SAGE PUBLICATIONS
Beverly Hills / London / New Delhi

For information address:

SAGE Publications, Inc.
275 South Beverly Drive
Beverly Hills, California 90212

SAGE Publications India Pvt. Ltd.
C-236 Defence Colony
New Delhi 110 024, India

SAGE Publications Ltd
28 Banner Street
London EC1Y 8QE, England

Printed in the United States of America

Library of Congress Cataloging in Publication Data

Main entry under title:

Evaluating your agency's programs.

   (Sage human services guides ; 29)
   "Published in cooperation with the Center
for Social Welfare Research of the School of
Social Work, University of Washington, and
the Continuing Education Program in the Human
Services of the University of Michigan School
of Social Work."
   Bibliography: p.
   1. Evaluation research. (Social action
programs)—United States. I. Austin, Michael J.
II. University of Washington. Center for
Social Welfare Research. III. University of
Michigan. Continuing Education Program in the
Human Services. IV. Series: Sage human
services guides ; v. 29)
HV91.S34 1982   361'.0068   82-10553
ISBN 0-8039-0989-6

THIRD PRINTING, 1985

CONTENTS

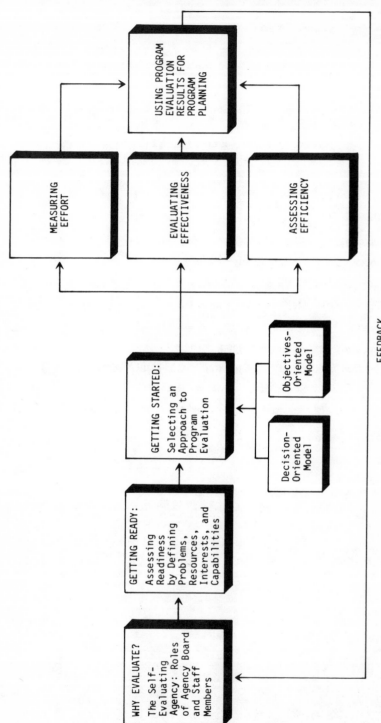

INTRODUCTION

If you are a board member of a social agency, you may have been called upon to evaluate your agency's programs and to make decisions and recommendations about new policies and directions. If you are a counselor or group worker, you may have wondered how effective your intervention activities have been and you may have been asked to justify your actions on the basis of results. If you are a program manager or agency administrator, you may have experienced frustration when seeking future funding support for your programs without the availability of relevant program evaluation data. These are issues which led to the development of this guide.

Different from other program evaluation guides, this book deals with the differing but complementary interests of board members, staff members, and administrators. It emerged from a two-year project that was sparked by the numerous requests received by the Center for Social Welfare Research, University of Washington School of Social Work, for assistance in evaluating the programs of small, United Way supported social service agencies. This guide seeks to place the relevant tools of program evaluation into the hands of agency staff and board members who are committed to working in a self-evaluating agency. A self-evaluating staff member represents the critical actor in conducting program evaluations in a self-evaluating agency. The book represents a blend between involving staff and board members in program evaluation and specifying the evaluation techniques and guidelines adaptable to a wide variety of social agency programs.

Without the knowledgeable support of an agency director and the active participation of agency board members, this guide might.sit on a shelf rather than on the desk of every staff member and in the possession of every board member. The active support and leadership of the agency director is needed in order to develop and maintain staff interest and commitment as well as board member participation. Administrators who are committed to the continuous search for new and better ways to deliver effective services to clients will no doubt actively encourage staff to engage in program evaluation activities, as well as demonstrate support by providing the necessary staff time to conduct program evaluations. Active support without the commensurate recognition that program evaluation takes time, and that it should be a part of every staff member's job description, can lead to staff frustration and alienation. The agency director along with the staff and the board are perceived as members of a three-way partnership, needed to shift program evaluation from an idea worth doing to a reality incorporated into the routine management of agency operations.

We have organized the guide into seven chapters. The first chapter includes introductory information found to be essential in helping an agency move from thinking about program evaluation to doing program evaluation. It is designed to answer two seemingly simple questions: (1) "Why conduct program evaluations?" and (2) "What is program evaluation?" Chapter 2 seeks to answer the question, "How do you get ready? Chapter 3 addresses "How do you get started?" These four questions reflect the most persistent concerns of agency staff and board members who are contemplating involvement in program evaluation activities.

The Chapters 4 and 5 include specific examples of how to apply evaluation methodologies by seeking answers to the following questions: (1) "How does a program coordinator or supervisor evaluate the effort of delivering services to a population of clients?" and (2) "How does a program coordinator or supervisor evaluate the effectiveness of such indirect services as outreach and prevention services?" These questions emerged from conversations with agency staff members who are confronted with the persistent need to make program decisions, now and in the future. Such decisions require information collected in an efficient and effective manner in order to make data-based decisions about the future. These two chapters can be supplemented by Appendix A and B, which include methods for single-case evaluation and selected program evaluation principles and practices such as question formulation, instrument development, data collection practices, and data analysis.

The last two chapters address another component of the decision-making process: evaluating program efficiency and linking program evaluation to program planning. Because few other program evaluation books include a discussion of the administrative issues, Chapters 6 and 7 were developed to answer three questions: (1) "How does one approach the process of assigning specific costs to particular programs?" (2) "How does one organize the program evaluation data into a system for future monitoring and assessment?" (3) "How does one relate program evaluation results to agency program planning?"

Each chapter was written by one or more persons who have had firsthand experience in conducting program evaluations. The process of translating such rich experience into the written word is not easy. The process of reading the chapters and translating the content back into your own daily practice will not be easy either. In some cases it may be useful for agencies to seek technical assistance after making some initial efforts to apply the contents of this book to the agency's unique needs. The key to the process of securing consultation, however, is the degree to which the agency specifies the relationship, not the other way around. A consultant should be utilized in such a way as to meet agency needs, including assistance in specifying evaluation questions, refining agency-developed questionnaires and instruments, assisting with the organization of evaluation data, and assisting with the interpretation and presentation of findings. The agency should define the nature of the service needed. We think that you will find this guide helpful in contracting with outside evaluators as well as useful in shaping the evaluations you will be conducting yourselves.

Our goal of developing a program evaluation manual requiring minimal technical assistance could not have been reached without the help of many people. Those helpers included Dean Scott Briar, Roger Thibadeau of the United Way of King County, Steven Mittenthal of the Weyerhaeuser Foundation, Mark Cooper of the Safeco Foundation, and the board members and staff of the following agencies: King County Association for Retarded Citizens, University YWCA, Renton Area Youth Services, Seattle Urban League Eastside Mental Health Center, Friends of Youth, and Youth Eastside Services. In addition, we acknowledge the helpful guidance of the Project Advisory Committee under the leadership of Nancy Cassill, including Leo Declos, Calvin Goerdel, James Leach, Donna McNamara, Jack Mullin, David Okimoto, Rita Ryder, Roger Thibadeau, Elizabeth Toth, and Bob Watt. We also acknowledge the outstanding assistance provided by our graduate students: Tom Berry, Steven Eckstrom, Chuck Foster, Christine Sabre, and the editorial assistance of Jill Crowell and Marcy Broder. And finally, we are indebted to Professor Armand Lauffer, editor of this series, for his excellent editorial advice and assistance.

WHY EVALUATE?

The Self-
Evaluating
Agency: Roles
of Agency Board
and Staff
Members

Chapter 1

WHY SHOULD AGENCIES EVALUATE
THEIR OWN PROGRAMS?

While the 1970s can be characterized as the age of agency accountability, the 1980s will most likely be the age of agency survival. The 1970s pressures for the documentation and evaluation of client services will continue as agencies seek to justify their existence. These trends have made it imperative that both the boards of directors and staffs of social service agencies understand the process of program evaluation. Only through evaluation can agencies make their programs credible to funding agencies and government authorities. In addition, program evaluation information can help the agency improve its services and become more responsive to the community. But who really cares most about using the results of program evaluations? What do you think? Mark your responses to the questions in Figure 1.1 by noting who you think cares most. Then take a minute and rank these items from 1 to 10 with 1 being the most important. Do it now and then go on. As you read further, you will be able to compare your responses to the perceptions of others.

Program evaluations rarely produce startling, unexpected results requiring major program change. In reality there are few such surprises, since good administrators and workers will be "in touch" with the results of their various programs and have a pretty good sense of what lies ahead. However, evaluation is useful in either confirming our suspicions or hunches or filling in some gap in our knowledge of how a program is working. In either case, we are talking about reducing uncertainty, not providing the final word.

| | | | | Who Cares Most? | |
| | | | | | Rank Order |
Selected Issues	Workers	Super-visors	Adminis-trators	Board Members	of Importance
1. Are the needs of the clients being met? (B)**	____	____	____	____	____
2. Are there sufficient resources to meet program objectives? (A)	____	____	____	____	____
3. Is the program too expensive? (C)	____	____	____	____	____
4. Should the program be expanded or curtailed? (A)	____	____	____	____	____
5. Is the service or treatment provided really effective? (B)	____	____	____	____	____
6. Are budget decisions about the future based on program evaluation data? (C)	____	____	____	____	____
7. Are we making best use of staff energy? (A)	____	____	____	____	____
8. Can evaluation data be used to compare program costs? (C)	____	____	____	____	____
9. What is the impact of a community forum series? (B)	____	____	____	____	____
10. What is the level of client satisfaction? (B)	____	____	____	____	____

*Place a check mark in one or more columns before rank ordering the importance of the ten questions.

**A = Effort; B = Effectiveness; C = Efficiency.

FIGURE 1.1 Checklist of Reasons for Using Program Evaluations*

REDUCING UNCERTAINTY

For example, suppose you are the director of a community education program in a youth service agency offering workshops for parents of teenagers on drug abuse, adolescent sexuality, and general parenting skills. You are pretty certain the program is effective in getting the ideas across, but you suspect this *knowledge* is not being translated into actual *behavior*. You decide to administer a questionnaire to the participants at a point two months after the workshops, and your suspicion is confirmed. The responses indicate that the participants are indeed learning the material, but the new knowledge is not producing any measurable change in family interactions. You need more information, however, in order to make appropriate program changes. You wonder if a closer look at the subjective experience of the participants might help. A next evaluative step might be to do some in-depth interviewing with a randomly selected group of participants, focusing on factors which inhibit behavioral change.

In yet another example, suppose that you are the director of a counseling program. You know your program is "successful" because clients are satisfied enough with the services and many return or frequently refer relatives and friends. You do not know, however, whether clients are really getting better in the long run. Are they able to cope successfully with their problems for a reasonable period of time after termination? Do they return with the same problems or new ones? What are the circumstances under which they return? You need an evaluative tool that will help you answer these questions.

In both of these examples, program evaluation is only one of many factors that may contribute to future changes. The community education director probably will not scrap the program because it may not be achieving its ultimate goal. The program serves other functions not measured in the evaluation, such as enhancing the agency's visibility and credibility in the community. Large-scale behavior change may be an unrealistic goal for this program, or it may be more important to focus on a special group, such as single-parent families, and develop follow-up interventions for them.

The counseling program director is also not expecting any surprises. While the total impact of effective counseling is difficult to determine, it is possible to document how the program serves as a resource for fulfilling important community needs. Knowing under what circumstances clients return to the program, along with specific client feedback, will help the counseling staff in directing their efforts and measuring the efficiency and effectiveness of the program.

Agency program decision making involves a process of gradual accumulation of information from many sources, leading eventually to program change. Program evaluation can assist the staff and board in identifying patterns and trends for the purpose of program planning and implementation.

EVALUATION FOR USE

The key to the successful use of evaluation is that it must be *designed to be used.* This may seem obvious, but in fact very little of the evaluation done today is actually designed to be used by agency staff. For example, in the community education example above, suppose a survey of parents participating in the parenting skills program revealed that (1) 70 percent "understand their kids better" than they did before, and (2) 20 percent feel that it "has had some impact" on their relations with their kids. Should we consider this a success? Or should these figures be higher for a program involving this much staff time? What about the difference between the two findings—can we live with this or do we want greater program impact on behavior? While these are good questions, they need to be specified *prior* to the implementation of the evaluation itself. The staff, administration, and representatives of the board should decide together what information is needed, the criteria for interpreting the results, and how the results will be used. In this way agency staff are encouraged to examine their expectations and to articulate implicit service goals and objectives.

In the case of the counseling program director who wanted to survey the clients' level of functioning after termination of service, it is important that clinicians and supervisors have input into exactly what information is gathered and how. If they are expected to use the information, they should be able to *believe* in it. They must be convinced that client self-reporting is valid in this situation, that a questionnaire is a good vehicle, that the particular questions being asked really get at the right issues, and that the timing of the evaluation is good. What would happen if such a survey revealed that a majority of clients "relapsed" after two months? If such a finding were to be taken seriously by staff, early involvement in the program evaluation process would enhance their confidence in the "validity" of the instrument and the findings. When agency staff and board members are not involved, program evaluation findings are likely to be ignored or rejected.

Just as evaluative data can give an agency administrator a more solid basis for his or her decisions and give the agency as a whole more credibility, so it can give workers more factual support and credibility within the agency. Direct service staff are concerned about their own effectiveness with clients and with their professional growth. Evaluation can help with both. It can provide hard data to add to the informal indicators of effectiveness, as well as to help identify certain needs for additional staff training. A counselor may sense that most of his or her clients are feeling pretty satisfied with the counseling when they terminate. A follow-up questionnaire might elicit some comments from clients to the effect that the counselor was less effective at helping them make decisions than learning how to express feelings. Are counselors concerned enough with skill development to want to make use of this kind of feedback? How important is it to become a self-evaluating worker? What is a self-evaluating agency? What are the attributes of the self-evaluating agency that need to be present if workers are to receive the necessary support for evaluating their practice?

THE SELF-EVALUATING AGENCY

The initiative to evaluate need not come from outside the agency. An agency can become its own best critic by evaluating itself and incorporating the results into ongoing program development. An agency that is committed to self-evaluation has little to fear from outside evaluators. The subsequent chapters should help you develop the self-evaluative capacity in your agency.

Self-evaluation begins with the commitment to improve programs in the context of limited resources available to social agencies. Self-evaluation is both an organizational principle and an economic and political necessity. Self-evaluation in the human services means the continuous monitoring and assessing of program activities, and the capacity and willingness to make changes based on the information gathered.

The self-evaluating agency is able to identify evaluation questions which need answers in order to make decisions sometime in the future. Are program goals and objectives being met? Even if they are being met, are they still relevant? Obviously, goals and objectives need to be written clearly in order to be measured and assessed for their relevance to client need.

Self-evaluation is an organizational principle because it determines a "way of life" for the organization as a whole. The commitment to self-evaluation affects all the actors in the organization, from clients to line workers, to supervisory and administrative staff, to board members and funders. It affects the emotional environment of the agency and its decision-making structure. It affects the agency's interactions with the external political environment.

Self-evaluation is a continuous process because program effectiveness can never be taken for granted. There are too many factors inside and outside the agency to assume that a program is meeting its goals. The needs of clients change, staff skills and interests change, patterns of acceptable behavior change, and accessibility of services also changes. The self-evaluating organization can equip itself to adapt to these changes by using the most current information to determine the direction of its program efforts.

Clients, staff, and board members must all be convinced of the value of developing a self-evaluating agency. While the practice of self-evaluation may in itself build internal support for policy changes, these critical actors must first become committed to the process. In order to create the trust necessary for ongoing self-evaluation, it is necessary to confront staff fears about losing jobs by rewarding staff with the necessary time and recognition needed for participating in critical self-assessment. While "change has its costs," an agency should guarantee its members the necessary job security and support needed to commit people to the evaluation process.

Trust is a key concept here. There must be a real commitment on all levels of staff to be open and responsive to evaluation results, whatever they may be. Self-evaluation includes determining the impact of a proposed change on the agency itself, not only on clients but on staff and board members as well. As Wildavsky notes (1972):

> The evaluative enterprise depends on common recognition that the activity is being carried out somehow in order to secure better policies, whatever these may be, and not in support of a predetermined position. If this understanding is violated, people down the line will refuse to cooperate. . . .
>
> A good evaluation not only specifies desirable outcomes but suggests institutional mechanisms for achieving them.

Like any organization, the self-evaluating agency must stabilize its environment and secure the loyalty of staff and board members, as well as outside funding support and goodwill.

All social service agency staff members hold a set of beliefs about what they think their agency is trying to do to meet a variety of client needs. Staff members also view clients from different perspectives (e.g., lazy, isolated, disturbed, lost, capable, normal). These beliefs help us to make sense of the complex web of human behavior and social environments. The beliefs include a set of implicit assumptions about the way we organize agency services to meet the needs of a client population. They suggest ways of conceptualizing client and organizational problems and solutions to these problems. This set of beliefs constitutes a service ideology. Raising questions about these beliefs represents an important ingredient in conducting program evaluations. The systematic approach to asking questions about the activities of agency staff requires considerable effort in order to make the beliefs explicit. This effort is critical if program evaluation is to become more than a self-serving process designed to legitimate the status quo.

By explicating beliefs about the goals of the agency in meeting the needs of clients, the staff in a self-evaluating agency are also able to share expectations about the standards they use for assessing the quality and quantity of agency services. This evaluating process often takes place in the minds of staff who look at the discrepancy between what should be happening and what actually is happening.

While program evaluation is not necessarily a search for discrepancies between service performance and service standards, it is a process that frequently uses standards to interpret evaluation findings. Effective program evaluation requires that staff seek to make explicit their service standards in order to ensure the use of evaluation findings in future decision making.

The self-evaluating agency is like a mature person. Some people and some agencies do what they are expected to do because the criteria are well-defined and the rewards or penalties for compliance are clear. However, when the criteria are not well-defined and the rewards or penalties are not clear, it is the mature and successful person who is self-directing in selecting goals and objectives. Being clear about the appropriateness and direction of one's efforts is another sign of maturity. Like a mature person, the agency which seeks to increase its autonomy for decision making, even if it is dependent or interdependent with many other organizations, is clear about where it is going and how it is getting there. An agency can make shifts and adjustments when necessary and thereby becomes less dependent on the rewards and penalties or standards established by others, even though it must respond to them. Therefore, a mature self-evaluating agency can respond to the changes in the external environment as well as to its own internal growth and development. Agency boards are often the link between staff and agency environment.

THE BOARD OF DIRECTORS AND
THE SELF-EVALUATING AGENCY

Most human service agencies are governed by boards, whether they are private voluntary agencies supported by the United Way or public agencies accountable to a city council or state legislature. Boards serve as policy-making groups which help determine the future directions of agency programs. Boards are frequently responsible for reviewing and establishing budgets, setting goals and objectives, hiring and firing the executive director, establishing personnel policies, monitoring the agency's effort and efficiency, assessing program effectiveness, and fund-raising. Through their interaction with people outside the agency, board members play a vital role in monitoring the reputation of the agency's programs.

Involvement in program evaluation may raise concerns on the part of board members as to the appropriateness of their role in the process. Board members may be concerned that stressing interest in evaluating the agency's program will be seen as a vote of "no confidence" in the director's ability. Another worry may be that evaluation would lower staff morale by making staff uncomfortable and resentful. Perhaps the toughest question is how program evaluation fits into the board's role in policy making, with the feeling that evaluation is something the staff and director should be doing. It is true that if the board decides to be involved in evaluation activities there will be less time to devote to other roles. The fact remains that evaluation efforts involving board members in developing question(s), supporting its implementation, and analyzing and interpreting the results are most likely to be successful in assisting staff to produce information that is useful for agency policy making.

MANAGEMENT'S ROLE IN PROGRAM EVALUATION
AND IN WORKING WITH THE BOARD

The agency director and other members of the management team need the support of the board in carrying out program evaluation. Unlike a service program, evaluation has no constituency and the products it provides are not as concrete or demonstrably useful as many service programs. At the very least, management needs support to reallocate resources to support the evaluation effort. The very act of adding a new evaluation activity to the management of the agency requires new roles and responsibilities for the board, staff, and executive. For example, deciding to evaluate a community education program in a youth service bureau may represent a new activity. Assuming that a subcommittee of the board will be involved, special meetings will need to be scheduled for both staff and board members. How will information be disseminated to the rest of the board and staff? Will there be a need for technical assistance at different times over the life of the evaluation study? Clearly a whole set of new communication channels are required in collaborative evaluation efforts by staff and board.

If staff are to be actively involved in developing the evaluation questions, in implementing the study, and in interpreting the findings, there needs to be recognition of these new activities. Incentives should be developed to gain staff commitment and involvement rather than the expectation that staff will add evaluation activities to an already hectic schedule. Staff may need convincing about the usefulness of the evaluation effort, if they are to be invested. They may want to be certain that the agency is serious about program evaluation and that such a commitment will be reflected in some changes in expectations as to how much time is spent in different job activities. The director can reflect the seriousness of the agency's commit-ment by putting in writing a contract, negotiated with workers, that outlines the amount of time that will be allocated to evaluation activities and corre-sponding decreases in hours in other service areas. Similarly, the board must decide on how to prioritize their different roles. One factor that will influ-ence how active the board becomes in evaluation is how important their other roles are to serving agency needs. For example, if fund-raising is the only activity considered worthy, they are not likely to invest much in program design and evaluation. But fund raising, like many other tasks, is limiting and does not make full use of the talents of board members.

Board members must be willing and should be expected to invest time and energy in identifying programs to be evaluated, monitoring the evaluation process, and assisting in interpreting the findings for policy decision making. The benefits of monitoring far outweigh the costs. Monitoring should not be viewed as a punitive "control function." We see it as a vehicle for the development of mutual understanding between board members and program staff.

Board involvement begins with deciding what program to evaluate and moves from there to a decision about how to help staff conduct the evaluation, including what types of evaluation questions to answer. Board members have a role to play in data analysis by checking to see if the analysis fits their information needs.

Board members of a self-evaluating agency view program evaluation as a part of board functioning as much as making budget recommendations or reviewing personnel actions. Requesting information on the effectiveness of services or efficiency of agency operations is a critical component of helping the agency achieve its mission. Actual board involvement in the evaluation process is greatest at the beginning, when the problem is being identified, and at the end in interpreting and implementing the results. Yet, together with the agency executive, board members can play an important role in supporting staff in implementing the evaluation. In fact, creating and maintaining an environment of mutual trust and support is the area where the executive needs to be particularly adept if the agency is to have a self-evaluating focus.

The self-evaluating agency cannot depend on boards and management alone. Central to the process is the "self-evaluating worker." Our image of the self-evaluating worker is a person who, in striving for some degree of objectivity and accountability in delivering services to clients, is professionally mature. This worker is committed to estimating and documenting reliably the effectiveness of his or her service intervention procedures. The purpose of an intervention may be to effect positive changes in a client's personal capacities and environment; the purpose of evaluation is to estimate the effects of the intervention on clients and their environment. It is difficult to engage in one of these activities effectively without engaging in the other. Clients, workers, and agencies all benefit from the self-evaluating worker.

The self-evaluating worker is capable of being explicit about several key aspects of service delivery: (1) able to describe different types of intervention (i.e., the ability to conceptualize practice methods); (2) able to describe the difference between service goals that are difficult to measure (i.e., improving the client's self-concept) and service objectives that are specific and measurable (i.e., client will feel more comfortable at job interviews); (3) able, willing, and comfortable in making estimations regarding the amount of time necessary to complete the intervention process; and (4) able to make evaluative judgments about case progress and admit that the service may not have achieved the objectives (e.g., "Yes, that case did not go very well; I must try a different approach next time.").

Who benefits from the worker's self-evaluation? Among those who benefit are the client, the worker, and the agency.

— The client gains from a sharper, more focused intervention. The worker's self-evaluation serves as a quality control mechanism by keeping up to date on each case through his or her own ongoing monitoring system.

— The worker benefits from the self-evaluation process when he or she uses the process as a system for monitoring the service delivery process. The evaluation process helps the worker to clarify what he or she is doing through documentation of how the case had started, where it is now, and where it might be going.

— The agency benefits from an ongoing client data system built by workers.

Another worker benefit is being able to look at documented success and share the documentation with co-workers and supervisor(s). The documentation clarifies and organizes what the worker has done and what the actual outcome of service delivery looks like. Through self-evaluation the worker is able to present clearly the uniqueness of the individual client or group and gain feedback about the presenting problem and the unique circumstances of the client's life. The worker can use the self-evaluation process as a self-correcting mechanism. For example, if the worker engages in a case evaluation and discovers that the service seems to be having a positive effect and is helping the client to change in mutually desired ways, the worker can then continue the service with confidence. Likewise, if the worker discovers that the service is not proving helpful to the client, different approaches or techniques can be utilized.

By describing and explaining service plans and activities, the worker gains a sense of direction. The evaluation process enables the worker to be clear about what he/she is doing and why. At the same time, clients can benefit from the positive effects derived from keeping track of their own progress. The clients can become more aware of what they are doing and why.

In summary, the definition of a self-evaluating worker presented here involves a number of aspects of the service delivery process. Self-evaluating workers need a thorough understanding of the methods they employ in a particular case, as well as confidence in asking questions about the effectiveness of the method. Self-evaluating workers know that evaluation is conducted for the sake of more effective service. Self-evaluating workers are also able to explain service goals and objectives, estimate the amount of time necessary for evaluating services, and demonstrate the commitment to evaluate services at a given point in time. The benefits resulting from the worker's self-evaluation process can be identified in terms of the client, the agency, and the worker. Perhaps the most vital aspect of self-evaluation is the commitment workers make to meeting service standards by documenting what they do in practice and why they do it.

Case Example of the Successful Use of Evaluation: "Evaluating Intake Services in a Youth Service Bureau"

The executive director of a multiservice youth agency appoints a program review committee to evaluate systematically the various program components and make recommendations for change. This committee consists of clinical, supervisory, and administrative staff and several board members. The director, who is the most knowledgeable about evaluation issues and techniques, acts as technical consultant. She directs them first to look at the intake service, since it is central to the whole "system" and because there has been considerable turnover of paid staff in that service program.

The committee decides they want to find out whether the intake service is working smoothly and efficiently, whether clients are getting the help they need and quickly enough, or if any are "falling between the cracks." They interview staff who work in intake; they also survey clients over a three-month period. The principal finding is that the half-time paid intake coordinator is having difficulty supervising a large volunteer staff, with consequent delays in client referral to counseling as revealed by the client survey. They also discover that intake workers are burdened with record-keeping (required by funders) which is often of no apparent value in providing services to clients. They recommend that the coordinator work full-time and that the extraneous paperwork be reduced or eliminated.

The executive director supports the first recommendation and plans to incorporate it into the next year's budget: the high turnover in that position has already alerted her to the possibility of this kind of structural problem. As for the second recommendation, she knows that the reporting requirements must be met, but wonders if the data gathered could be made more relevant to intake staff or streamlined in some way. She directs the review committee to study this issue further.

We have chosen this example in order to emphasize the fact that program evaluation need not be overly complex to be useful, that it does not necessarily involve an elaborate methodology. What *is* important is the level of involvement of staff in design and implementation and that the thrust for evaluation, and hence for change, comes from within the agency itself. Evaluation also represents an ongoing trial-and-error process. Not all the results are conclusive or useful, but the self-evaluating agency is committed to the process of steady and systematic review and improvement of services. Program evaluation can focus on a variety of agency activities including clinical evaluation, financial assessment, and prevention services. While the focus may differ greatly, the following four steps are common to any evaluation effort:

1. Identifying and organizing the decision makers.
2. Determining the focus of program evaluation.
3. Designing the procedures for collecting information.
4. Gathering, analyzing, and interpreting the data.

Each of these steps involves the staff and board to varying degrees. Clearly, the board needs to be involved heavily in steps one and four, and to a lesser extent in steps two and three. On the other hand, staff needs to be involved equally in all of these steps.

1. IDENTIFYING AND ORGANIZING THE DECISION MAKERS

The first and perhaps most crucial step in program evaluation is identifying the relevant decision makers and information users—that is, those who are in a position to use information, to whom it "makes a difference," who have questions they want answered, and who are therefore willing to share responsibility for the evaluation and its actual use. The decision makers include workers, program coordinators, supervisors, administrators, and board members.

In addition, there must be some structure, a team or task force, which allows for regular and direct contact between these information users and the staff members who coordinate the actual evaluation process. This group should be small and willing and able to make a time commitment to the evaluation process. In the case of clinical services, for example, the team may consist only of the supervisor and a few workers. It is important for those involved in self-evaluation to have structured opportunities to gain support and assistance from one another.

Principles to Remember. Be sure that (1) those you expect to do self-evaluation are involved in the decision about what to evaluate, and (2) those whose decisions count when evaluative information is examined are involved, and involved early.

---

2. DETERMINING THE FOCUS OF PROGRAM EVALUATION

The focus of program evaluation depends on the kinds of problems facing the board, executive, and/or staff which require additional information. One way to look at information needs is to think in terms of program effort, effectiveness, or efficiency. In the checklist noted at the beginning of the chapter, questions were raised relating to the different uses of program evaluations. Each question was coded according to the focus of the evaluation questions (e.g., A = Effort; B = Effectiveness; and C = Efficiency) and it would be useful to review those questions.

DEFINING EFFORT (A)

Effort questions are concerned with the inputs into a program; with the amount and kinds of program activities used to achieve program results. Effort refers to staff time and activity, the allocation and use of material resources such as office space and equipment. When a question is raised to uncover what and how much an agency program is doing to reach a desired end, an effort question is being asked. Effort questions will yield answers that will tell you, for example, the number of clients served, the amount of staff time on various activities within a program, and the number of service contacts per month. This kind of information does not tell you how well the activities are being carried out, but it does indicate that something is happening. Most agencies collect information about effort in order to comply with the accountability requirements of funding sources.

DEFINING EFFECTIVENESS (B)

Board, executive, and staff usually want more than just information about effort. They also want to know something about the effectiveness of a program. For example, did the special Group Home for youth meet its objectives of preventing delinquency? Has the behavior of program participants been changed in some way? Measurements of effectiveness are concerned with results, expressed as information about program outputs and client outcomes. Effectiveness questions can yield information about the impact of a program on its participants, its staff, and the agency.

In focusing on effectiveness issues, it is important to beware of unanticipated program consequences, consequences that are not expected to result from programs' efforts. For example, an unanticipated consequence of drug abuse prevention education programs may be the sharing of new information with youth who decide to experiment with drugs based on the education program. Thus, the unanticipated consequences of a program that is viewed as effective may include increased drug abuse.

Critical to effectiveness evaluation is the use of comparisons. A client's behavior may be compared before and after treatment. Rates of delinquent behavior may be measured prior to, during, and after the completion of a delinquency prevention project. The attitudes of participants in a series of drug education workshops may be compared before and after the sessions. A group of clients receiving one kind of treatment may be compared with a similar group of clients receiving yet another kind of treatment. Clients with different presenting problems receiving similar services may be compared to see if one kind of client responds to treatment better than another. It is comparisons like these that help to assess the effects of a program on its participants.

DEFINING EFFICIENCY (C)

The third perspective on program evaluation is efficiency and the productive use of resources to meet program goals and objectives. Efficiency speaks to the relative costs of achieving program results, such as personnel, time, money, and physical facilities.

Efficiency questions seek information on the effort of a program in comparison to its effectiveness. How much effort was expended for what result? How much "bang" did we get for our dollar? Answers to these kinds of questions will yield information, for example, on the dollar costs per program participant per outcome of service. How much money did it cost the agency for clients placed in jobs compared to those who have yet to find work? Efficiency questions focus on more than just dollar costs. They may focus on time or facilities. Can we reduce the amount of time it takes to do an intake interview? How can the office be rearranged to utilize existing space better? How can we define staff roles better to meet our objectives? Is there duplication of effort?

Regardless of its content, an efficiency question seeks information on the relationship between program inputs (effort) and program results (effectiveness). Efficiency questions are often raised in times of limited resources when service decisions need to be made, such as emphasizing services to groups rather than individuals, or contracting out to someone who can do it cheaper and with apparently better results.

Thus, effort, effectiveness, and efficiency are three useful concepts in determining the agency's information needs. Each type of question will yield different kinds of information. Each kind of information will paint a slightly different picture of the program under study, and each picture may lead to different decisions. The amount of weight given to evaluation information will, of course, depend on the immediacy of the decision and the context of that decision. If there are sufficient agency resources, effectiveness might be the only guide. If there do not seem to be enough resources, special weight may be given to effort and efficiency information.

The decision to study either effort, effectiveness, or efficiency, or all three helps sharpen the focus of evaluation. And it helps the agency decide how to

a. evaluate programs where a decision to continue, modify, or terminate must be made;
b. evaluate programs where a shortage of information makes decision making difficult;
c. evaluate programs where information will make a difference (if political and interpersonal realities will cause the evaluation to be ignored, forget it);
d. evaluate programs where data are readily available or can be generated easily; and
e. evaluate programs where costs will not exceed information gained (e.g., is the cost of the evaluation worth it?).

Principles to Remember. In developing the evaluation focus: (1) It should be a program evaluation problem about which it is possible to gather data in the first place; problems which are too broad (we don't know if we are making people healthy) or too sensitive (we aren't able to tell if clients' sexual behaviors change as a result of our intervention) are probably not the kinds of questions about which we can gather meaningful data. (2) There must be more than one possible response to the problem, in the sense of informants being really free to express their views. For example, to ask a youth who is in a court-ordered counseling program whether she is "satisfied" with the service is probably a bad question: She will be aware that her "success" in the program is keeping her out of an institution and is not likely to say anything that might jeopardize her status. (3) The identified decision makers must *want* and *need* more information than is already available. If they believe they already have enough to go on, or if they prefer to rely on informal feedback mechanisms that have served them well before, then evaluation is a waste of time. (4) The decision makers must want information for *themselves* and not just to satisfy external funding demands. Finally, (5) it is crucial that these decision makers be able to articulate how they would use the results of any information gathered to address the problem.

3. DESIGNING THE PROCEDURES FOR
COLLECTING INFORMATION

The next major step in the evaluation process is to choose a methodology that will generate *useful information*. The world of methodology is often viewed as a technical nightmare in which measurement issues appear hopelessly complex. Nevertheless, the choice of how to gather data to address the evaluation question is an important one and should be addressed by staff. It is not enough for the evaluation questions to be relevant; the method for gathering information must also be relevant. The dominant model in evaluation draws on social science techniques of pre- and posttesting, comparison or control groups, and standardized measurement instruments. These techniques are described in subsequent chapters.

An evaluation that does not get close enough to a program to perceive its "inner life" is not likely to be seen as useful by those involved in it. For example, not all the benefits of an innovative educational program will show up on a standardized test; not all the benefits of a youth employment program will show up in reduced juvenile crime. The subjective element is also important because it relates to the legitimacy of the evaluation as perceived by the potential information users. The teacher in an innovative educational program will have little trust in an evaluation that looks only at test results and neglects the quality of interaction in the classroom; the supervisor of a youth employment program will pay little attention to an evaluation that measures only recidivism and neglects the program's potential for enhancing self-esteem. On the other hand, the board of education may trust test results only in making program decisions, and the federal government may be interested only in recidivism rates when making decisions about future funding.

For program evaluations conducted in the changing environments of social agencies, it makes no sense to impose a strict experimental design, requiring control groups, on a program whose goals are frequently not spelled out and whose interventions are frequently being adjusted to changing needs and demands. Far more useful would be a design that records the *process* of the program as it develops and feeds back to the staff information that will contribute to this development. In a follow-up study of clients after termination from counseling, the best evaluation strategy may involve gathering as much information as possible on individual cases as they become available. Since it is likely that some counselors will be more open to having the success of their work scrutinized in this way, it would be less threatening to the rest of the staff to begin by looking only at the cases of those staff who are amenable to evaluation. Perhaps generalizations will come later as more counselors perceive the value of this kind of study and as more data accumulate.

In choosing an evaluation methodology it is also important to monitor the reliability and validity of evaluation instruments and designs. Reliability refers to the standardized nature of the measurement instrument (such as a test or a questionnaire) which assumes that it will produce consistent information across different applications. If the questionnaire items are worded vaguely, so that respondents are confused about the meaning, responses will be arbitrary and erratic, producing an instrument that is not reliable. On the other hand, validity refers to whether or not you are really measuring what you want to measure. It is quite possible that respondents will answer a given question consistently in a way that is different from what the evaluator intended and consequently the results would not be valid. While both reliability and validity are obviously desirable, the self-evaluating organization should pay special attention to validity because it relates directly to the immediate *usefulness* of the data.

Principles to Remember. Program evaluation decisions should be shared with staff in order to enhance their understanding of, belief in, and commitment to the results. The design must be *credible* to all concerned. Staff members should be familiar with some of the strengths and weaknesses of different ways of collecting data and be able to make choices within the constraints imposed by limited resources, limited time, and the accessibility of data. To sum up, *it is better to have a probable and approximate answer to the right question than a solid and certain answer to the wrong question.*

---

4. GATHERING, ANALYZING, AND INTERPRETING THE DATA

After the evaluation questions have been developed and the methodology chosen, the next step is to collect the data and then analyze and interpret them. The activities for data analysis and interpretation include the following eight steps:

ANALYSIS

1. Compilation of data	2. Organization of data	3. Comparison of data	4. Raising questions about data

INTERPRETING FINDINGS

5.	6.	7.	8.
Developing viable answers to questions about data	Developing program policy options for each answer	Developing recommendations (prioritizing options)	Converting recommendations into action plans

In a self-evaluating agency, staff are involved in analyzing and interpreting findings. While assistance might be sought in organizing the data analysis process, interpretation should be a separate process in which staff are involved. To interpret information is to attach meaning to it. Interpretation is greatly facilitated if all concerned go into the process agreeing on what "success" might look like. In any program evaluation the staff will offer their own interpretation of the data. Board members should be given the opportunity to do the same, without the intrusion of the staff's judgements. The more board members become involved in the interpretation of program evaluation findings, the more they will become aware of the multiple interpretation of these findings.

Principles to Remember. The emphasis should be on what the data indicate about specific situations and relationships, rather than on judging the program as "good" or "bad." Involved staff will see more clearly the strengths and weaknesses of the data and know better how to interpret the findings. The interpretation process involves making inferences from data, moving from analysis to action, and in the self-evaluating agency this is a joint effort of board, direct service, and administrative staff.

SUMMARY

This chapter has stressed the importance of conducting program evaluation, particularly the "self-evaluating agency's" model of self-initiated program monitoring and change. We addressed some of the organizational issues raised by this model, such as the need for job security and trust. In describing the uses of evaluation we emphasized its potential as one of a variety of tools for agency decision making. Self-evaluating workers and involved board members are the key actors.

One major issue that emerges from our discussion is the need for an organizational environment characterized by mutual trust, honesty, and willingness to be self-critical. We firmly believe that in the long run, the self-evaluating capacity of an organization fosters such an atmosphere. We also recognize that for many organizations it seems as if some kind of "leap of faith" is required to get there. The trust we are talking about cannot be created overnight, and yet it seems almost a necessary precondition for adopting an evaluative stance. This is why we have stressed the importance of involving all levels of staff in evaluation design, implementation, and interpretation.

This chapter also included the four major steps in the program evaluation process: (1) identifying and organizing the decision makers, (2) determining the focus of program evaluation (e.g., effort, effectiveness, and efficiency), (3) designing the procedures for collecting information (e.g., pre- and post-tests, follow-up studies, comparison or control groups, and use of standardized measurement instruments), and (4) analyzing and interpreting the data.

The next chapter, on assessing your agency's readiness for program evaluation, represents the bridge between this chapter on identifying the rationale and steps of program evaluation and subsequent chapters on specific evaluation techniques.

REFERENCES

ATTKISSON, C. C. et al. (1978) Evaluation of Human Service Programs. New York: Academic Press.

GRUBB, C. (1976) Program Evaluation and Local Administration. Chapel Hill, NC: Institute for Social Service Planning.

HASENFELD, Y. and R. A. ENGLISH [eds.] (1974) Human Services Organizations. Ann Arbor: University of Michigan Press.

PATTON, M. Q. (1978) Utilization-Focused Evaluation. Beverly Hills, CA: Sage.

WILDAVSKY, A. (1972) "The self-evaluating organization." Public Administration Review September-October: 509-520.

WOLFENSBERGER, W. and L. GLENN (1975) Pass 3: A Method for the Quantitative Evaluation of Human Services (field manual, 3rd edition). Toronto, Canada: National Institute of Mental Retardation.

YAVORSKY, D. K. (1976) Discrepancy Evaluation: A Practitioner's Guide. Evaluation Research Center, University of Virginia.

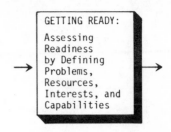

GETTING READY:

Assessing
Readiness
by Defining
Problems,
Resources,
Interests, and
Capabilities

Chapter 2

GETTING READY

Nearly everyone claims to recognize the need or value of program evaluation, even while they grumble about doing evaluations which are seen as a waste of time or yielding meaningless results. Clearly, some evaluations have been a waste of time and do yield meaningless results, not only because the evaluation questions or methods were poor but also because the agency and staff just were not ready to use program evaluation seriously or meaningfully. Readiness is determined, in part, by wanting to learn and being able to make use of what is learned. It requires a degree of confidence in one's current ability to use the current resources of time and money to generate more resources in the future. It requires leadership, both the technical kind to do the evaluating and the normative kind necessary to establish a perspective which values the process, the results, and the utility of evaluations. We shall begin by examining how you can tell if the agency and staff are ready for evaluation.

AGENCY READINESS FOR EVALUATION

An agency's readiness to engage in evaluation activities is based on many factors including time, money, attitudes, morale, and leadership. Before reading further, please complete Figure 2.1. It should help you determine your own agency's readiness. Ideally, board members, staff members, and the director should complete it independently. Later on you may want to use the checklist in a group discussion as a way of making more accurate assessments of agency readiness. Asking agency staff and board to respond individually may be helpful in determining areas of agreement and disagreement. Irrespec-

I. Answer each of the following questions by checking yes or no.

	Yes	No
1. There are sufficient financial *resources* to support an evaluation effort in the agency.	_____	_____
2. Staff workloads can be reallocated to allow *one person to coordinate* a program evaluation process.	_____	_____
3. The agency has a *planning structure* that can be used to help implement the study and use its findings.	_____	_____
4. The *timing* is good, in terms of staff morale, for an evaluation effort.	_____	_____
5. The staff have demonstrated the ability to take *risks* in trying new ways of doing things.	_____	_____
6. The director has demonstrated an ability to *manage change.*	_____	_____

II. Board members, staff, and the director may hold different views of the following statements. Check each statement in terms of your views of how each group or person might respond, including your own view, if you are a staff member, for example.

	Yes			No.		
	Board	*Dir.*	*Staff*	*Board*	*Dir.*	*Staff*
1. Conducting a program evaluation is consistent with the *agency's philosophy.*	___	___	___	___	___	___
2. Program evaluation is seen as a threat and sign of *distrust.*	___	___	___	___	___	___
3. Most people connected with this agency have little *interest* in program evaluation.	___	___	___	___	___	___
4. Program evaluation is seen as providing some *useful information* to the agency.	___	___	___	___	___	___
5. Agency *staff* have the *capability* to carry out the evaluation.	___	___	___	___	___	___
6. The *benefits* of an agency self-evaluation exceed the costs of time and money.	___	___	___	___	___	___

FIGURE 2.1   Assessment of Agency Readiness for Program Evaluation

tive of the outcome of the readiness discussion, a written statement should be prepared for the board of directors indicating readiness or lack of readiness and why.

Agency resources are key factors in carrying out an evaluation. Program evaluation is not without costs. Resources must be allocated to support the activity. Staff, board, and executive time will be needed at various steps in the process. Since agency staff need to be heavily involved in carrying out the evaluation, some staff time might be taken away from delivering services to clients. Consultant or technical assistance may be needed at different points in time depending on the size and complexity of the evaluation.

Unfortunately there is no way to attach an exact dollar figure to different kinds of program evaluation. However, estimates of staff time and support services can be made. For example, seeking consumer satisfaction information through the development of a survey might require between five and eight meetings of staff to determine the contents, develop the instrument, and review the field-testing of the instrument. A consultant might be enlisted to review and critique the instruments. If more than 50 clients are to be surveyed, the data could be computerized and statistically analyzed. Evalua tion studies usually involve photocopying and typing costs, along witl postage for mailed surveys. The staff coordinator of a program evaluation needs to plan for the time needed to develop instruments, organize the data processing, analyze the data, and write the reports.

Coordination of staff and board by one individual or a small work group charged with the responsibility is key to ensuring a successful evaluation process. The individual or work group should be staff members with sufficient credibility to be respected by the staff and board. Identifying one person or work group with the overall responsibility signals the importance of the activity to all agency participants, provides a resource for questions or concerns, and creates strong incentives for that individual or work group to become invested in the evaluation process.

An existing planning structure that involves agency staff, board, and executive will be in a better position to implement the findings from an evaluation study than will an agency which does not plan ahead. If the planning process is in place, there is a clear structure for the results of the evaluation to be used in planning future programs. Otherwise, new organizational structures to support planning and evaluation will be needed. Additional information on the relationship between program planning and program evaluation is noted in Chapter 7.

Timing is a critical factor in determining an agency's readiness for change. A program evaluation may begin in April and findings may not be available until December. Implementation of decisions on the basis of evaluation findings must consider the effects of the passage of time on a program.

Ideally, evaluation procedures should be built in at the very beginning of a new project or program. Procedures and forms for collecting data that are built in from the start are less likely to be resisted. Another factor that affects timing is the condition of the agency's goals and objectives. If board and staff are in the process of refocusing the agency's mission or developing operational goals and objectives, evaluation would best be done when these activities are completed. The specification of clear goals and objectives are helpful in setting the direction and focus of program evaluations.

Risk taking requires trust, cooperation, and supportive relationships. Are workers encouraged to make suggestions in areas where they see a need for improvement? Are people rewarded for trying new and innovative ways of handling a situation? Is change in programs seen as a positive force or is it dismissed as more trouble than it is worth? Answers to these questions will give clues to how open and willing workers will be to trying something new. A supportive agency climate is crucial for staff to take chances and perform new evaluation tasks.

The *executive's skill in managing change* is an important factor in assessing readiness for program evaluation. Regardless of the quality and expertise of the staff, there is bound to be resistance from at least some of the staff. Resistance may be stronger among volunteer staff than paid staff, failing to see the value of evaluation or simply unwilling to donate their time to a task requiring more paperwork. How the executive is perceived and his or her ability to manage resistance, help coordinate activities, give clear directions, and facilitate the work of staff are crucial. An administrator who displays initiative, a willingness to try new ideas, and an ability to follow through, will greatly enhance the success of implementing evaluation recommendations.

Agency philosophy can also influence evaluation efforts. If there is a heavy emphasis on client privacy and confidentiality, a followup study of consumer satisfaction may not be possible. Other approaches to evaluation are possible despite the fact that an agency's philosophy about client services may make it difficult to answer some questions of interest.

Similarly, program procedures and practices growing out of the agency philosophy may present obstacles. For example, a congregate care facility or halfway house where staff place great emphasis on creating a communal, family-type atmosphere may not be conducive to the use of a battery of evaluation instruments at the beginning and end of a resident's stay. This same dilemma holds true for evaluation at the individual level. A clinician with a strong psychodynamic approach may feel that an emphasis on measurement and documenting behavior interferes with the development of a relationship with the client. Chapter 3 points out many alternative approaches to doing clinical research which could address this concern.

Staff distrust may accompany initial discussions of agency program evaluation (e.g., "Why are they evaluating my program?" "Are the results going to be used against me?"). One factor that will influence the level of staff distrust is the agency's history of collecting data. If the agency has a history of gathering information for the purpose of punishing individuals or eliminating programs, then the distrust is well-founded. The feelings of distrust, incompetence, and disinterest all represent potential sources of resistance. It is important to assess the strength of these feelings and perceptions before proceeding with an evaluation effort.

Program evaluation is a new idea for many agency staff members, board members, and directors. It evokes many different feelings and perceptions. *Lack of interest* may be linked with feelings of individual incompetence. For example, a staff member hired to deliver individual and family counseling services may resent the time required to participate in program evaluation activities and, therefore, may not be interested in learning new evaluation techniques. Staff members may feel incompetent when it comes to program evaluations. They may feel considerable tension between their recognition of the need for accountability and their commitment to serve clients. Chapter 3 identifies how case-by-case evaluation can be an integral part of service, but many practitioners may not see it that way.

User expectations represent another variable to consider. Board members, executives, and staff members need to have some belief that program evaluation can answer questions and provide useful information to the agency. Suppose an agency starts a new program serving groups of high school students who need to improve their problem solving and communication skills. This program may require reduced counselor time spent on individual and family counseling. If the agency is trying to decide whether to continue the group program, staff may see evaluating the effectiveness of the two kinds of groups as a way to make a decision. However, if the director does not see it as an open question but rather a political one, then it makes little sense to do an evaluation whose results will not be used to change the mix of services. Program evaluation needs to be seen as a viable option by individuals involved in the effort. They should have some faith in the evaluation methodology and tools, and a readiness to use the answers.

Not only does program evaluation need to be seen as a means for assessing program effectiveness, but there needs to be some agreement that a problem or question exists. If the executive is deeply committed to a drug prevention program and strongly feels it is working well, there may be little reason to spend time doing an evaluation of the results. Similarly, if direct service counseling staff do not believe it is possible to accurately capture students' attitudes toward a group counseling program through a paper and pencil form, it makes little sense to spend time developing a questionnaire on consumer satisfaction.

Staff capability relates to a willingness to learn and/or the existence of previous training. A background in evaluation research or even a familiarity with some of the common tasks, such as operationalizing terms and documenting behavior changes, can be helpful. Staff capability also refers to the amount of time available to carry out evaluation activities. If caseloads have just increased by 10 percent and staff were already feeling overloaded, the time may not be available for conducting an evaluation.

The benefits or payoff from the evaluation activity should be assessed by board members, staff, and executive. If the program evaluation effort is to determine the effectiveness of family counseling, then the clinician and the supervisors will need to see that the benefits are greater than the costs. Similarly, if the effort is aimed at making program cost information more useful in planning, then the executive and board members will need to recognize the relative advantage of the information. However, when the evaluation is of a program which looks at the outcome and cost of client services, everyone in the agency needs to see and appreciate the benefits.

It is difficult to be certain in advance whether or not a particular evaluation effort will result in information that is "worth" more than it cost in terms of time, energy, and money. The value placed on evaluation is a subjective decision. What makes this factor important is that the perceptions of the payoff will influence the support, energy, and quality of effort in carrying out the process. Unless there is some agreement, particularly on the part of the individuals implementing the program that the evaluation questions are important, there is little reason to proceed.

If reading about the different factors important to a successful evaluation effort has left you thinking your agency is not ready, it may be important to plan some pre-evaluation activities. Go back to the checklist you filled out earlier in the chapter. Statements with "no" responses may suggest the need to do some preliminary work. If you are the director, you may need to work with the board on developing a board training workshop or attend some evaluation workshops yourself. If you are a staff member, you may need to work with the director on ways to encourage more staff input into agency decisions as an important pre-condition to stimulating involvement in conducting a program evaluation. Regardless of your position in the agency, the checklist can be used as a tool to deciding on whether to start on an evaluation or on pre-evaluation activities. The following vignette describes an agency which sought to assess its readiness for program evaluation.

Case Example: *"Client-Outcome Evaluation"*

Valley Community Services for the Mentally Disabled was becoming increasingly concerned about the lack of information on client outcomes. Another agency in the city had recently submitted a grant proposal offering to deliver services very similar to those that the funding agency had contracted with Valley Community Services to provide during the past year. This new source of competition, coupled with the lack of data demonstrating client change, provided a condition supportive of evaluation efforts.

For some time the board had received program information from the executive and staff. Numbers served, frequency of client contacts, and similar effort information had been available on their in-house chore services program. The program evaluation subcommittee of the board and director recognized that a successful effort required a staff person assigned to oversee the project and act as a link between board, staff, and director. The director was willing to detail Diane, the assistant director, to the effort as one of her major tasks over the next six months.

The subcommittee expressed the greatest interest in knowing more about the in-home services program. The program involves a chore service person working with clients and assisting in helping them develop daily living skills. This was considered a stable program, having been funded in large part by United Way for the past five years. While there was a good deal of turnover in chore workers, the two social workers, who performed the assessment of clients and helped to establish service goals, had been with the program for a number of years, and looked forward to the challenge of conducting an evaluation.

The already strong emphasis on operationalizing client goals made the research notion of developing *measures* less threatening and consistent with agency philosophy. While earlier evaluation efforts had been limited to collecting simple summary statistics, the board and staff expressed an interest in assessing program effectiveness.

Though staff had an interest in being able to measure client change better, it was clear that their enthusiasm would last only so long as an instrument improved their practice. Recognition of this fact meant that the necessary staff involvement could probably be obtained if staff were assured that the assessment instrument would replace the current procedures and would actually ease their work. There existed enough agreement among the board, executive, and staff about the importance of the question of client change that the self-evaluating model seemed more useful than hiring an outside consultant. Staff had caseloads which appeared stable, and so were in a position to allocate some time to evaluation activities. Given this set of circumstances, the agency director decided the agency was ready to get started.

Principles to Remember. This is a "do-it-yourself" page. Review the case illustration and the discussion that preceded it. Jot down the principles that you think apply. Now add other principles that emerge from your own agency experience.

Assuming that an agency and staff have determined that they are ready, the next step is getting started. In the following chapter, two models for getting started are described.

REFERENCES

ALKIN, M. C., R. DAILLAK, and P. WHITE (1978) Using Evaluations: Does Evaluation Make a Difference? Beverly Hills, CA: Sage.

CHASE, G. (1979) "Implementing a human services program: how hard will it be?" Public Policy 27, 4: 385-435.

DAVIS, H. (1973) "Planning for Creative Change in Mental Health Services: A Manual on Research Utilization. DHEW Publication No. (HSM) 73-9147. Washington, DC: Government Printing Office.

NEWMAN, H. and A. VAN WIJK (1980) Self-Evaluation for Human Service Organizations. New York: Greater New York Fund/United Way.

RUTMAN, L. (1980) Planning Useful Evaluations: Evaluability Assessment. Beverly Hills, CA: Sage.

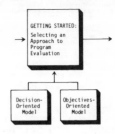

Chapter 3

GETTING STARTED

This chapter introduces two methods for getting started on program evaluation: the decision-oriented model and the objectives-oriented model. Each model approaches evaluation from a slightly different perspective. You may find one approach more appropriate or useful depending on your particular agency circumstances. Neither model is necessarily better than the other, and you may want to combine various aspects of both approaches. We begin with the decision-oriented model.

The decision-oriented model is based on the assumption that program evaluation is useful primarily if it seeks to answer questions related to a current or future program decision. For example, if the staff and board see the need for a decision, in a year, on whether or not to expand the outreach or "meals on wheels" program, then the planning of a program evaluation process should be linked to such a decision. The second model is a program objectives-oriented model that is based on the assumption that objectives have been clearly specified and the future decision, raised each year, relates to the question, "How well is this program meeting its objectives?" This model presumes that evaluation will or has become a routine part of agency life. As you can see, the first model is more inductive and raises the question, "What do we need to know in order to make a decision in the future?" The second model is more deductive and raises the question, "Since we have been committed to these objectives over the past few years, how do we know if we are meeting them and if they are still releant?" The decision to choose one of these models should be made at a joint meeting of selected staff and board members. Each model will lead you into the evaluation process from a slightly different perspective.

GETTING STARTED BY USING
THE DECISION-ORIENTED MODEL

This model is built on a Four-Step Decision-Making Guide for determining the agency's information needs in order to arrive at more informed decisions related to effort, efficiency, and effectiveness. The following four steps are based on answering the basic questions of what, where, how, and who:

Step 1: *What* is the problem and who cares?
   - Defining the problem requiring a decision in the future.
   - Who is concerned and why?
   - What information is needed?

Step 2: *Where* can we get the necessary information?
   - How confidential is it?
   - Who is least likely to be interested in providing the information and why?
   - What resources do we need to get the information?

Step 3: *How* good will the information be?
   - What measures are needed to ensure the quality of the information?
   - Can we use existing documents and information collection instruments?
   - Do we need to create new instruments?
   - How frequently should the information be collected and reported?

Step 4: *Who* will collect and report the information?
   - How will the information be reported and summarized?
   - Who will assess the validity and reliability of the information?
   - How will the information be fed back for decision making?
   - How will the utility of the results be assessed?

We have found that an effective method for using this guide is to involve staff and board members in the review of such questions. You might begin this process by filling in the blanks in Figure 3.1.

Step 1: *What* is the problem and who cares?

In some cases specifying the problem clearly is not difficult. The board of a residential treatment agency might state the following problem: "In order to make informed program changes we need to know which parts of the program are useful or not useful" (effectiveness). A clinician's problem might initially be stated as "I don't know how to assess the outcome of my group treatment program for people with substance abuse problems" (effectiveness) or "I'm seeing a lot of chronically mentally ill people with so many needs I

(text continued on page 44)

Step 1: What is the problem and who cares?

	1.	2.	3.	4.
	What is the problem to be solved?	Who cares about the problem?	Why are they concerned? What do they want to do?	What information is needed to solve the problem?
1.				
2.				
3.				

FIGURE 3.1 Four-Step Guide for Determining, Assessing, and Meeting Information Needs

Step 2: Where can we get the necessary information?

	5. Where could we get the information? Who will provide it?	6. How confidential is the needed information?	7. Who is likely to be least interested in providing needed information?	8. Why are they the least interested?	9. What resources will ensure its collection?
1.					
2.					
3.					

FIGURE 3.1 (continued)

Step 3: How good will the information be?

	10. How good will the information be?	11. What measures should be used?	12. What source documents/collection instruments should be used or created?	13. How frequently will information be collected?
1.				
2.				
3.				

FIGURE 3.1 (continued)

Step 4: Who will collect and report the information?

	14. Who will collect and report the information?	15. How valid and reliable is the information likely to be?	16. How will information be fed back? (Format)	17. What is the utility of the information in solving the problem?
1.				
2.				
3.				

FIGURE 3.1 (continued)

43

don't know how best to allocate my time to be most effective" (efficiency). In both of these cases, it is important to specify the problem more clearly in order to set the direction for the evaluation process.

Vagueness is not the only source of difficulty in specifying the problem to be solved. Some problems can be seen from different perspectives and would lead to the collection of different kinds of information. This is why it is helpful to include all the users of the evaluation findings in all the steps of the evaluation process.

For example, the board of a youth services agency needed to reach a decision on the allocation of funds to a group counseling program and individual counseling program. Some saw the problem in terms of which program provided the higher level of reimbrusement from outside funding sources, while others saw the issue in terms of which program provided the most effective treatment. While at first glance the problem was seen as straightforward, several meetings were needed to specify the problem clearly.

If it is difficult to think of a specific problem, it may be easier to begin the process by developing questions you might have about a particular program. The questions might relate to the kinds of services offered, the cost of providing different services, or other issues which decision makers need to address in charting the agency's course. The key criteria for assessing the relevance of the question is its relationship to a decision that needs to be made *and* the need for additional information. Many questions might not produce the relevant information for decision making. Developing a problem statement or asking a question are two ways of beginning the process. Subsequent chapters describe the process of developing questions for the evaluation study and the role of a problem statement.

Who cares about the problem and what do they want to know? This question seeks to identify those who think this is a problem. Clarifying the audience helps clarify the type of information needed. If, for example, you were collecting information on the allocations of staff time for funding sources, you might use only general program information. If, on the other hand, you want to use information for managemenf control decisions about allocating resources to different programs, then you need to determine how individual staff are allocating their time. If possible, it is best to begin with a question of interest to staff. In so doing, you most likely will be answering questions of interest to outside funding sources as well as the board of directors.

What do *they* want to know? This question seeks to identify how things would look if you were to solve the problem successfully. Another way to put it is, "What goals would we reach if we solve the problem?" Suppose your problem was not knowing what happened to clients who were referred to employers through your job development and referral service. Program staff might want to know who is being hired and for what kinds of jobs, in order to plan for further job development activities. If your answer to this question results in a list of information that is not currently available and would take more time than appears worthwhile, you may want to reconsider your original question at this point and reformulate it to be more specific in pinpointing your concern more accurately.

What information is needed to solve the problem? The response to this question is crucial in setting the direction of the evaluation study. In the previous example of the Youth Services Bureau Board of Directors, the allocation of staff time between individual and group counseling was seen by some as a financial issue that would involve information related to rates of reimbursement and allocating costs to the different treatment methods. On the other hand, if the problem was defined in terms of treatment effectiveness, then the response would relate to measuring client changes and outcome in relationship to allocated staff time.

Step 2: *Where* **can we get the necessary information?**

Alternative sources? Your agency's documents in the form of client records or budgetary information are common sources of information. For example, if your interest is in the outcome of a peer counseling program, there might be a number of alternative information sources such as school records of referrals to the office for disciplinary problems, student self-reports of vandalism, violence, or drug use, or official police or court records. For financial information, the bookkeeper is one of the sources. In the case of monitoring work activity of day care staff, the staff members themselves would need to be involved.

How confidential is the needed information? In some cases this question is most important. If your goal is to gather information on arrest rates and disciplinary reports on children who have gone through a peer counseling program, you may have trouble getting information due to laws on confidentiality. Not only must you consider the matter of access to the information, but once you have sensitive data on individuals, plans must be made to ensure protecting the identities of clients. It is also helpful at this point to consider whether you can promise clients or staff anonymity or confidentiality if they agree to participate in a study. The issue of research ethics is discussed more fully in Appendix B.

Who is likely to be least interested in providing needed information? One of the biggest problems in trying to collect and use information systematically is that, frequently, the people who have the least interest in collecting information are the very people who are expected to collect it. It is not unusual for staff, who are involved with their clients day in and day out, to feel that some forms of documentation are unnecessary. As one child care worker remarked, "I'm always working on changing kids' behavior and I know what works and what doesn't. So I don't see any point in keeping track of behavior changes. I know when they happen." For direct service staff, collecting information is done usually at the expense of time spent with clients. Therefore, it means time away from a more challenging, exciting task. One other factor that can explain why staff would not want to collect information is the fear of what the data would show and how they would be used. Some client populations, such as those referred by court order, may have little motivation to respond to a consumer satisfaction survey sent to them after treatment.

What resources will ensure the collection of needed information? In order to ensure that data are collected, staff could be required to collect them or clients could simply be reminded frequently to fill out the follow-up forms. Both of these methods are likely to lead to a poor response or certainly increase the probability of invalid data. It is important to prepare staff and/or clients by identifying the importance of the information, how it can help the agency, and the need for accurate and periodic reporting. This point relates to managing change and will be discussed later.

Step 3: *How* good will the quality of the collected information be?

Some information may be more valid than other information. Confidence in the information may vary by source, so in filling out the checklist indicate "good," "fair," or "poor" with regard to each information source. The response to this step depends on how successfully you carried out the previous steps.

What measures should be used? This is a key question and relates directly to the problem to be solved (Step 1) and the information needed to solve the problem (Step 2) to make a decision about measures to be used. Frequently, people fail to make a logical linkage between the problem to be solved and the measures used.

The problem of inappropriate measures is most common in evaluating program outcomes, and this problem is exacerbated when intended program outcomes or objectives are ambiguous. Without specifying the logic and assumptions that underlie the treatment program and what treatment is intended to accomplish, it is likely that people will be measuring things that have little likelihood of being changed by the services offered. For example, drug knowledge questionnaires used to assess the outcomes of an affective-education approach to drug abuse prevention may be measuring the wrong thing. There is little reason to expect that an affective education program will increase drug knowledge, so the measure is inappropriate. Measures can be aimed at documenting attitudes, behavior, feelings, amount of direct and indirect costs, and a host of other areas of interest to decision makers.

What source documents or data collection instruments should be used or created? Just because you have decided on the measure does not mean the collection instrument is determined. For example, you may feel it is important to find out how satisfied participants were with your five-week lecture series on parent effectiveness. Yet, there are a number of different ways to collect the information: telephone interviews, face-to-face interviews, or group feedback sessions, to name a few. In addition, it is important also to consider information that already exists. Such a source may be the number of participants attending more than one lecture, as evidenced by names on the registration list. In order to get the information you need, you might also consider the possibility of revising an existing form that is also used for other purposes. Along the same line, if an external source requires information, think of how those data can be collected in order to be useful in answering the questions of interest to you.

When and how frequently will information be collected? Often the goal in program evaluation is to gather information that is representative of all clients in a program or of staff activities on all days of the week. Therefore, it is useful to think of the possibility of time sampling. If you are interested in documenting staff activity, you might ask staff to keep a record for a different day each week for five weeks. This makes the recording less tedious and can increase reliability of the records.

Step 4: *Who* **will collect and report the information?**

Answers to this question will vary greatly with the problem. A school social worker interested in determining if there is a pattern to the truancy of one of her clients may summarize the information in a bar graph for each week. In some cases, the best time to summarize the data will be obvious. For the five-week series on parent effectiveness, it would make sense for the program director to write a summary at the end of each of the individual sessions. Financial information is most likely to be summarized and prepared at regular monthly, quarterly, or annual intervals.

The length of time for reporting information may vary for different groups. The director may get a report at the end of each series of community lectures, but the board may get a summary only at the end of the year. Similarly, the person assigned to summarize the information on children's use of privileges in a residential treatment center may share the results weekly in staff meetings but report it only monthly or quarterly to the director.

How valid and reliable is the information likely to be? This question is aimed at getting you to stop and think about the quality of data you are going to collect, primarily with regard to what is going on in the program (validity) and the consistency with which the evaluation instruments are completed (reliability). Staff training may be necessary in order to assure the accuracy and consistency of the collected information. Periodic discussions with staff may be needed to reinforce the importance of accurate reporting and data collection.

How will the information be fed back? From the beginning, it is helpful to reach agreement on the form of the reports, including the type of information to be included and the format. In order to make sure the data will be used as fully as possible, all those receiving the report should be consulted on the most usable, easiest understood format.

What will be the utility of the information after three months? With some problems, this question will need to be asked only once. If you are doing an outcome study of the effects of two different treatment approaches, the utility of the information will be related to the specific study itself. However, if data collection activities are aimed at developing an ongoing, continuous information system to be used for agency planning and programming, it becomes important that this question be asked repeatedly at different intervals to ensure the same information is still desired.

By this time you should have a good understanding of the factors which signal "go" or "no go" in making the decision to conduct a program evaluation study. In addition, having worked through your questions or problem of interest, you now have a clear picture of the tasks and individuals involved in responding to the problem. You should be prepared to use one or more of the subsequent chapters on evaluation methodology and data analysis techniques. In order to demonstrate the utility of this decision-oriented model, the next chapter provides a detailed elaboration of all the steps related to evaluating prevention services. The following vignette illustrates one agency's experience in working through the four steps.

Case Example: "Working Through the Four Steps"

The board and director at the Valley General Community Services all agreed that it was time they tried to grapple with the question of the effectiveness of their in-home program. Questions of this kind were raised in an internal memo sent to board and staff. It read in part:

> To what extent do our programs facilitate skill development or simply sustain people at their current level of functioning? To what extent would the findings be a reflection of our programming or a reflection of the limitations of the populations we serve? Answers to these questions directly affect our long-term planning for where we want to be in three to five years.

Further discussion by a subgroup of staff and the program evaluation subcommittee of the board led to the specification of the problem as "We don't know what kind of change clients are experiencing in our programs"

(Step 1). This was a problem of interest to all agency participants, who, for different reasons, felt the need for information to guide program efforts.

Board members could use the information in determining the mission of the agency. The director would be able to use the evaluation process demonstrated in the In-home Living Skills Program in looking at other agency programs. Direct service staff would be in a position to determine those skill areas where chore workers were having the greatest success and greatest difficulty in helping develop client's skills. This information would place them in a position of trying new methods in those problem areas shown to be resistant to change.

Responses to Step 2 suggested that a number of sources could be useful. Relatives, families, hotel and apartment managers, in addition to staff, could offer useful information. Tests could be administered to measure behavioral changes in lots of areas. Brief reports from families and friends could be used to try to capture the client's functioning before entering the program and a second measure for present functioning. Client records would be another source. Thus, social work staff and chore workers in the program would be involved in the study. Since only existing staff would review the records, confidentiality was not a problem. Since the social workers responsible for collecting the data believed that more accurate information would be very helpful in their job, they did not need to contend with the problem of people unwilling to collect data. Ensuring collection of the needed information was effectively handled by the assistant director, along with the director, who gave evaluation activities a high priority.

Staff, board, and director all displayed confidence in getting accurate information from a behavioral rating scale (Step 3). Since there was little turnover in the program, with only three or four new clients becoming involved each month, there was a need for information from individuals that could describe the individual's functioning at the time of starting the program. Measures to be used included creation of an assessment tool which covered all social living skills. Also, a brief survey was used in phone interviews to a family member, relative, or landlord in a position to describe the person's functioning before entering the program. The assessment tool would be completed every six months for each client.

Given the wide range of client factors to be assessed and the desire to work on relationships among different skill areas, the agency decided the information needed to be put on computer tapes. Therefore, it was agreed that staff would code their assessment responses and an individual would be hired to keypunch and program the data. The computer programmer would be responsible for providing a summary of data based on direct service staff and director's information. Information would be shared with the board every six months.

Asking themselves (Step 4) "How valid and reliable is the information likely to be?" forced staff to think of the limitations of the validity of the data. By no means would they have proved that their service was the cause of changes in the client's behavior. Changes in clients could be a result of other factors, or may reflect changes in the social workers performing the assessment rather than the clients. Only a controlled experiment could definitely come to this conclusion. Yet despite these reservations, the proposed plan remained the best possible way to get information that would help in making program decisions. While the social workers recognized the limitations of their study, reflecting on the limitations also made clear some techniques they could use to improve the study. Since two different social workers were going to be involved in performing assessments, staff recognized the need for working together to help ensure giving the same rating for a particular skill level. In this way the reliability of the measures could be markedly improved.

How the information was to be fed back to agency participants varied by position. Staff were interested in data not only in aggregate form but also on each individual case, so any patterns across individuals could be observed. Therefore, the computer programmer agreed first to send individual and aggregated data to staff, who, in conjunction with the assistant director, would review the information and, in turn, pull together the aggregated statistics which board members requested and needed for decision making.

The proposed plan included using the assessment tool every six months. Especially after getting another set of observations, staff agreed that it would be wise to take another look at the instrument and consider modification as needed.

The responses to the four steps in this vignette also demonstrate how to use the remaining chapters in the book. If it is necessary to assess program costs, then the chapter on evaluating program cost would be a logical place to go. Techniques for gathering information about changes taking place in treating groups of clients can be found in the chapter on formulation questions. On the other hand, if you need to develop a questionnaire on client satisfaction or conduct a needs assessment, then the chapter on data collection strategies would be helpful. Assistance in developing data collection instruments for monitoring individual client behaviors as part of treatment can be found in the chapter on evaluating services to individuals and families. And finally, if there is a need to collect and store data over a period of time, the chapter on evaluating program efficiency should be useful.

We have now completed our description of the four step *decision-oriented* model for beginning the program evaluation process. As noted earlier, it is an inductive model which raises the question, "What do we need to know in order to make a decision in the future?" In order to give agency personnel a choice, we have suggested a second approach, the objectives-oriented model, which is based on the assumption that program objectives have been clearly specified and that future decisions are based on the question, "How well is this program meeting its objectives?" The objectives-oriented model is deductive, in that it seeks to answer the question, "Since we have been committed to these objectives over the past few years, how do we know if we are meeting them and if they are still relevant?" It is important to understand both models before selecting one and starting your own program evaluation process.

GETTING STARTED BY USING THE
OBJECTIVES-ORIENTED MODEL[1]

In the previous section we described the use of a decision-oriented model for program evaluation. This section introduces an alternative method, called the objectives-oriented model, which can be used to evaluate a program. As noted previously, the two approaches can be contrasted in the following way:

1. The *decision-oriented model* is an *inductive* process which raises the question, "What do we need to know in order to make a decision in the *future*?"
2. The *objectives-oriented model* is *deductive* and seeks to answer the question, "Since we have been committed to these *objectives* over the past few years, how do we know if we are meeting them and if they are *still relevant*?"

The objectives-oriented model assumes that program evaluation takes place within a particular agency designed and established to meet the service needs of clients. To address client needs, the agency has clearly articulated its structure and function to include (1) agency mission or purpose, (2) program goals, (3) service activity objectives, and (4) tasks related to case objectives. The structure and function relationship can be envisioned as follows:

Structure	*Function*
AGENCY—————————————	MISSION
PROGRAM —————————————	GOALS
ACTIVITIES —————————————	PROGRAM OBJECTIVES
TASKS —————————————	CASE OBJECTIVES

The objectives-oriented model will be illustrated with a step-by-step process similar to the description of the decision-oriented model. The six-step process is highlighted below and is followed by a discussion of each step:

Step 1:   What is the agency's mission statement?
— Are the community problems which the agency seeks to address clearly identified?
— Are the target populations to be served identified?
— Are the desired results from providing services specified?
— Are the service approaches (e.g. counseling, educating) described?

Step 2:   What are the program goals?
— Does each of the program's goal statements describe the *activities* designed to meet the goals, the clients to be served, program staffing patterns, and program budget?
— Does each of the program's goal statements describe the *desired impact* in terms of the client population, the problems to be addressed, and the service delivery approaches?

Step 3:   What are the program objectives?
— Is each program goal related to a set of measurable objectives for activities necessary to achieve the goal?
— Are *process* objectives addressed in terms of how services are delivered?
— Are *impact* objectives specified in terms of assessing the impact of services on clients?

Step 4:   How do we determine whether program objectives have been met?
— What measures can be used to determine the extent to which program objectives have been met?
— Have we utilized both process and impact measures?
— Do our activities relate to meeting the program's objectives?

Step 5:   How do we determine whether client service objectives have been met?
— Have specific service objectives been developed *with* the client?
— Have the approaches to be used to reach these objectives been specified?
— Are periodic assessments made of clients' progress toward meeting objectives?
— Do workers and supervisors make periodic assessments of their own effectiveness by reviewing the progress of their caseloads?

Step 6:   How can we use program evaluation results?

- Have the findings been carefully organized to interpret the degree to which program goals and objectives have been achieved?
- Have we allowed enough time for the interpretation process to unfold?
- What factors (both internal and external) seem to account for the evaluation findings?
- What program changes should be considered in light of the successes and areas in need of improvement?
- How will the findings, interpretations, and future plans be shared?

As with the decision-oriented model, the most effective method of using this guide is through an initial *joint* meeting of staff and board members to begin the process of reviewing and answering the identified questions. Emerging from an initial meeting would be the following:

1. The formation of a work group consisting of staff members and one or more representatives of the board, led by an appointed or elected chairperson and recorder.
2. The development of a work plan with deadlines for the completion of each step in the model.

Our discussion begins with Step 1. In practice, it will be important to complete each step of the model satisfactorily before proceeding with the next step.

Step 1: What is the agency's mission statement?

The program evaluation process can begin with a review of your agency's mission statement or set of purposes, which are usually located in an annual report or in the agency's original articles of incorporation as a nonprofit organization. The mission statement should include answers to the following questions:

a. Are the social problems which the agency seeks to address clearly identified?
b. Are the target populations to be served identified?
c. Are the desired results from providing services clearly specified?
d. Are the service approaches (e.g., counseling, educating) clearly described?

If these statements are not up to date, relevant, or acceptable, they should be modified before proceeding with the next step of the process. At this early stage it is also important to discuss the range of potential findings that might emerge from the evaluation and how such findings would relate to future decisions. Brainstorming the development of potential scenarios is a central feature of getting started.

Step 2: What are the program goals?

Once the agency's mission statement has been reviewed and/or modified, the program goals related to the agency's range of services should be reviewed. Program *goal statements* should include the desired outcome, client population, problems addressed, and service delivery approaches. Provided below is an example of a program goal statement which includes these four elements:

> To achieve self-sufficiency (desired outcome) for developmentally disabled residents of the community (client population) by enhancing their average daily living skills (problems encountered) by providing a complete range of counseling, educational, and occupational services (service delivery approaches).

Each goal statement should also include descriptions of

1. activities designed to meet the goals of the program (i.e., education, health care, parent involvement, etc.),
2. clients to be served (e.g., preteens, teens, young adults, adults, elderly),
3. staffing patterns (e.g., director, counselor, case aides), and
4. program budget (e.g., sources of income for the program and types of program expenses).

Figure 3.2 can be used to relate program goal statements to program descriptions.

Step 3: What are the program objectives?

Each program goal should have a related set of objectives which are seen as necessary for achieving the goal. Developing program objectives involves the identification of two types of service activities: process activities and impact activities.

Process activities relate to the internal operation of the program: (1) the effort expended (e.g., staff time) and (2) the efficiency of the effort (e.g., relationship of the average time it takes to complete an activity and the volume of work to be done or clients served). An example of a process objective is provided below:

> To reduce the average time it takes to complete an intake interview by 25 percent by October 1, 19 ___ .

Impact activities relate to the desired impact of a program activity on a client or client group following the delivery of service. Impact activities,

I.   *Range of Program Activities:*

II.   *Range of Clients Served by Program:*

III.   *Range of Staff Involved in Delivering Program Services:*

IV.   *Program Budget, Including Income Sources and Types of Expenses:*

     INCOME   *EXPENSES*

V.   *Goal Statements for This Program:*

 A. Desired outcome:

 B. Client population:

 C. Problems addressed by program:

 D. Service delivery approaches:

 E. Complete program goal statement:

FIGURE 3.2   Program Description and Program Goals

therefore, address the issue of program effectiveness. Here is an example of an impact objective:

> To enable 65 percent of the adolescents diagnosed as developmentally disabled to achieve self-sufficienty (e.g., self-care skills and job-related skills) before reaching the age of 21.

With the completion of Steps 1, 2, and 3, you will have clear descriptions of your agency's mission, goals of a specific program, and the objectives of a specific program. Only at this point are you ready to consider ways to measure the extent to which goals and objectives have been achieved. In other words, without specifying goals and objectives, there is no basis for using this model for program evaluation.

Step 4: How do we determine whether program objectives have been met?

Determining the extent to which program objectives have been achieved requires the collection of systematic feedback. What information do we need to help us understand the relationship between program activities and program objectives? Do our activities produce results that lead to the accomplishment of the program objectives? To obtain feedback with respect to program objectives it is necessary to develop evaluation *measures* for assessing both process and impact objectives.

Process measures are usually defined in terms of three different indicators: workflow, volume, and productivity.

1. Workflow can be measured in terms of *client time* (e.g., average time between call for appointment and the appointment, between beginning and completion of intake, between intake and admission, between admission and discharge or termination) and/or *worker time* (e.g., average time to complete writeup of intake, average time to complete discharge planning, average time to complete job skills education program, average time to complete crisis referrals).
2. Volume can be measured in terms of number of *clients served* (e.g., weekly, monthly, annually) and/or the number of *services provided* (interviews conducted, meals served, in-patient days, counseling sessions, home visits, etc.).
3. Productivity can be measured in terms of performance ratios related to *costs, staff,* and *time.* Costs can be related to units of service or activities (e.g., cost per counseling session, classroom training session, diagnostic assessment, discharge planning, etc.). Staff ratios can be related to workload standards (number of cases per counselor, number of participants per class, number of community information meetings per worker, etc.). Time ratios can be related to the frequency of a program activity in a given time frame (e.g., number of clients screened for eligibility per month, number of counseling sessions per week, number of training or activity sessions per day).

Impact measures are frequently viewed as both the most important and the most difficult measures to develop and use. Ideally, you should seek out and use existing measures or instruments that have been tested for their validity (e.g., does it measure what it says it measures?) and reliability (e.g., does it work for different populations and with repeated usage?). However, very few existing measures meet the needs of staff, as well as program objectives. Therefore, you may need to invest the time and energy to develop your own measures. There are at least four types of impact measures which you can develop: (1) client satisfaction questionnaires; (2) client knowledge, skills, and attitude questionnaires; (3) questionnaires for significant others; and (4) behavioral observation checklists.

1. Client satisfaction questionnaires can be developed to measure the client's views of the activities which were designed to meet the objectives of the program (e.g., perceptions of intake, counseling sessions, educational sessions, worker effectiveness, agency accessibility, service availability).
2. Client knowledge, skills, and attitudes (KSA) questionnaires can be developed to assess the client's capacity to learn or meet the objective: of educational activities. Such self-administered questionnaires can be used to measure effectiveness, as well as to serve as a learning device for the participant.
3. Assessment of client outcome can also be measured by means of a questionnaire or interview of the client's significant others (e.g., spouse, parent, employer, friend). This approach, like all the others, obviously requires the consent of the client.
4. Behavioral observation checklists can also be developed as a measure of the client's capacity to utilize the KSAs acquired through educational activities or insights and learned behaviors acquired through counseling activities. Since the development of this measure requires considerable skill, consultation from local experts is advised.

A guide has been provided in Figure 3.3 for the specification of program objectives and program measures. Needless to say, a program includes more than one objective for process activities and for outcome activities. We suggest that you identify more than one measure for each objective. In reality it may be too time-consuming to use all of your suggested measures for each objective. However, the process of identifying multiple measures will help you acquire as complete an understanding of process and outcome as possible.

The last component of program evaluation relates specifically to the client. This level of evaluation draws on the worker's skill in specifying educational, treatment, or services objectives *with* the client, in order to engage in an activity that meets the learning, socioemotional, or coping needs of the client.

I. Program objective for a process activity:	Workflow indicator (client/time worker time):
	Volume indicator (clients served/ services provided):
	Productivity ratio (cost ratio, staff ratio, time ratio):
II. Program objective for an outcome activity:	Client Statisfaction:
	Assessment of client knowledge, skills, and attitudes (KSA):
	Assessments of significant others:
	Observed client behaviors:

FIGURE 3.3   Program Objectives and Program Measures

This approach to evaluation has at least three components: (1) specifying realistic objectives for the client to achieve within the context and time frame of the program, (2) specifying the approach to be used to reach the objective (e.g., behavioral counseling, psychodynamic insight counseling, didactic instruction, experiential instruction), and (3) periodic assessment of the progress made to reach the client's objectives.

Based on this approach, workers can reflect the progress made toward reaching the objectives in the form of graphs, as reflected in Figure 3.4. These graphs can be assessed by looking at all such progress measures across a worker's caseload of clients or classroom of participants.

While supervisors frequently assess a worker's caseload or an instructor's participant population for evaluating the level of worker performance, it is also possible to look across a caseload or classroom population to assess the impact of the service at regular intervals. This form of program evaluation by caseload represents one of the most important components of program evaluation for the self-evaluating agency. Any conscientious self-evaluating agency requires an equally conscientious self-evaluating staff.

Step 5: How do we determine whether client service objectives have been met?

Steps 1 through 4 of this model focus on the achievement of objectives at the program level. Step 5, in contrast, relates specifically to the client service objectives. This level of evaluation draws on the worker's skill in specifying educational, treatment, or service objectives *with* the client in order to engage in an activity that meets the learning, socioemotional, or coping needs of the client. This component of evaluation has at least three major activities: (1) specifying realistic objectives for the client to achieve within the context and time frame of the program, (2) specifying the approach to be used to reach the objectives (e.g., behavioral counseling, psychodynamic insight counseling, didactic instruction, experiential instruction), and (3) periodic assessment of client progress toward objectives.

Using this approach, client progress toward meeting objectives can be charted using graphs such as those illustrated in Figure 3.4. The methods for conducting single-case evaluations are described in detailed in Appendix A. Workers can use single-case evaluation, not only to monitor an individual client's progress but also to assess their own effectiveness as they review their entire caseload of clients or classroom of participants. This form of program evaluation by case represents one of the most important components of program evaluation for the self-evaluating agency.

Step 6: How can we use program evaluation results?

It takes considerable time, effort, and commitment to clarify goals and objectives, as well as to develop and implement meaningful evaluation mea-

I.   Client objectives:

II.   Service approach:

III.   Frequency of monitoring client progress:

IV.   Frequency of monitoring caseload or learner population progress:

V.   Sample Graphs:

       Client objective: To increase the number of daily conversations between
                            depressed adolescent and parents.

Frequency of Alice's Conversations with Parents When Depressed

FIGURE 3.4   Case Objectives and Case Measures

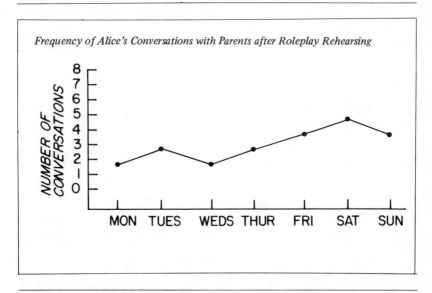

Frequency of Alice's Conversations with Parents after Roleplay Rehearsing

FIGURE 3.4 (continued)

sures. If your agency staff and board members have completed Steps 1 through 5, you will have made significant headway. To complete the objectives-oriented model, Step 6 is required to put the evaluation results to use. It is one of the most demanding steps of the evaluation effort and requires creativity, thoughtfulness, and persistance. It may also be a highly charged emotional experience based on differing interpretations of the findings. It is at this point when you will ask, "How do the findings relate to the achievement of our objectives?" Putting evaluation results to use consists primarily of two stages: (1) interpreting the findings, and (2) translating the findings into action steps for program planning and improvement. Each of these stages is discussed below.

Interpreting the findings. The first step in putting results to use is to *organize* the findings in such a way as to make the interpretation process a shared and open activity. We recommend first that the findings be jointly reviewed and interpreted by staff and board members. We also suggest organizing the findings into two categories: (1) anticipated and unanticipated results, and (2) positive and negative results, as noted in Figure 3.5.

Clearly, these are emotionally charged categories. What may have been anticipated by one staff member may not be anticipated by another. Similarly, viewing positive and negative results may be exciting to one staff

I.   Agency mission statement:

II. Program goal statements:

III. Program objective statements:

	Positive Results	Negative Results
Anticipated		
Unanticipated		

FIGURE 3.5   Organizing the Findings

member and depressing to another. Findings are often viewed from the
perspective of personal feelings, commitments, and frames of reference (e.g.,
is the bottle half full or half empty?). Irrespective of the emotional feelings,
findings require thinking and pondering, and therefore time is needed for this
interpretation process to unfold. For staff members who are disturbed by the
findings, as well as for those exhilarated by them, it is critical that all participants in the evaluation process seek answers to these questions: "Why
did this finding emerge?" "Do we need to look more closely at the nature of
the service provided?" "Do we need to refine our measures?" "Do we need to
specify our objectives in more detail?"

Whatever the answers, the key to the effective use of program evaluation
results is the process of inquiry. Learning to improve or change something
requires open and free exploration of alternatives. This dynamic is the essence
of accountability and the foundation for program development and change.

This foundation provides the essential rationale for conducting program evaluations. How are we doing? Can we do better? Where do we need to focus our energies? How do we collectively utilize feedback from the program evaluation process in order to make this agency an interesting place to work and a reputable community resource? These questions lead to the final step of program planning and improvement.

Translating findings into action steps for program planning and improvement. In this final step of the evaluation process, and with your interpretation of the findings in hand, you are now ready to translate the findings into action steps for program planning and improvement. The set of questions below can help guide this process. In seeking answers to these key questions, it is important to distinguish between internal factors (factors emerging within the agency) and external factors (related to influences outside the agency) which may affect both your understanding of the findings and their implications for future action.

1. If the program accomplished its goals and objectives, what were the primary reasons?

Internal Factors - objectives set too low, therefore easy to reach
  - effective methods or approaches used
  - staff competence and commitment adequate
  - adequate resources

External Factors - changing nature of client population
  - assistance from other agencies
  - new funding available

2. If the program did not reach its goals and objectives, what were the primary reasons?

Internal Factors - unrealistic goals and objectives
  - activities focus on symptoms, not causes
  - lack of staff expertise
  - inadequate measures

External Factors - reduced funding
  - changing community expectations
  - changing client population

3. What program changes should be considered in light of the successes and areas in need of improvement?

Internal Factors - increase/decrease activities
  - change methods of service delivery
  - upgrade staff
  - reward staff

External Factors - seek more funding
                  - advertise successes
                  - use areas in need of improvement as evidence of
                    honest self-assessment

4. How will the findings, interpretation, and future plans be shared?

With other staff?
With the board of directors?
With other agencies?
At conferences?
In the professional journals?
In the local press?
With clients?

CONCLUSION

This chapter was designed to help board and staff members think through the steps necessary for getting started on program evaluation. It follows a chapter on the "getting ready" stage where issues of financial resources, coordination, timing, planning, risk-taking, and management are addressed. Once it is clear that your agency is ready for program evaluation, the next step involves selecting one or both models for getting started. This chapter presented two such models: the decision-oriented model and the objectives-oriented model.

The decision-oriented model includes four steps: (1) What is the problem and who cares? (2) Where can we get the necessary information? (3) How good will the information be? and (4) Who will collect and report the information? This model is useful for agency personnel who seriously question the relevance and utility of evaluation. The model allows for open discussion of the key issues that must be addressed in the getting-started phase if the results of the evaluation are to be useful.

The second approach is the objectives-oriented model. This model is built on the assumption that agency personnel have clearly specified program goals and objectives and are interested in getting the evaluation process started. In this model, staff and board members carry out the following steps: (1) review the agency's mission, (2) document program description and goals, (3) specify program process activities and measures, as well as outcome activities and measures, (4) specify case objectives and case measures, (5) organize the findings related to anticipated and unanticipated positive and negative results, and (6) interpret the results in the context of program planning and dissemination. The next two chapters will provide an opportunity to see these two models in action.

NOTE

1. Adapted from Newman and Van Wijk (1980).

REFERENCES

ALKIN, M. C., R. DAILLAK, and P. WHITE (1978) Using Evaluations: Does Evaluation Make a Difference? Beverly Hills, CA: Sage.

CHASE, G. (1979) "Implementing a human services program: how hard will it be?" Public Policy 27, 4: 385-435.

DAVIS, H. (1973) Planning for Creative Change in Mental Health Services: A Manual on Research Utilization. DHEW Publication No. (HSM) 73-9147. Washington, DC: Government Printing Office.

NEWMAN, H. and A. VAN WIJK (1980) Self-Evaluation for Human Service Organizations. New York: Greater New York Fund/United Way.

RUTMAN, L. (1980) Planning Useful Evaluations: Evaluability Assessment. Beverly Hills, CA: Sage.

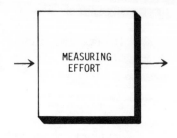

Chapter 4

MEASURING PROGRAM EFFORT

In this chapter we provide you with a detailed example of how to apply the decision-oriented and objectives-oriented models described in the previous chapters. We will show you the relationship between effort and effectiveness. Effectiveness will be addressed more thoroughly in the next chapter. In order to build an information base for measuring program effectiveness, it is useful to design a process for measuring effort. As we noted earlier, measuring effort involves the documentation of staff time and energy invested in delivering services. This measurement activity is frequently referred to as monitoring. Monitoring can include the recording of quantitative (e.g., how many clients did we serve?) as well as qualitative information (e.g., how well did we do?). We have chosen to use the evaluation of prevention services (one of the most difficult services to evaluate) as a case example for documenting effort. We see the documentation of effort as a first step in reaching decisions on the approach needed to measure effectiveness.

Preventive services seek to head off a problem *before* it occurs, while treatment services are provided after a problem has been recognized. Preventive services often focus on altering the environmental conditions that contribute to such problems as delinquency, drug abuse, child abuse, and physical illness. In seeking to change the contributing and causal conditions, preventive services can be provided in three ways:

1. *Direct Services to Target Populations.* These are services to people or groups who may, at some point, experience or contribute to the problem of concern. These may be general populations, such as all the students in a school, parents in PTA group, or high-risk populations, such as low-income children who need a head start in order to prevent

future educational problems. Other examples of direct services are community information and education programs or nutritional hot meal programs for senior citizens.

2. *Indirect Services.* Training and consultation are examples of indirect services provided to such groups as teachers, mental health workers, or police officers so as to help them become more effective in delivering preventive services (e.g., teacher-effectiveness training or drug information classes for law enforcement officers).

3. *Institutional Change Activities.* Activities focus on altering organizations, institutions, policies, or laws to decrease the likelihood that social and organizational conditions will cause problems. Examples include efforts to change grading practices in schools, legislative lobbying to decriminalize juvenile status offenses, and efforts to reorganize the work place to reduce stress.

The notions behind preventive services are appealing. It makes sense to try to prevent problems rather than simply waiting for them to happen. Some people argue that preventive approaches should cost less per individual served than treatment services, which must remediate damages that have already occurred. Yet the evaluation of preventive services is not easy. To show that preventive services are effective, it is necessary to show that something did not happen that would have happened had the services not been provided.

When preventive services are not provided directly to individuals, evaluation becomes even more difficult. For example, community-organizing projects seeking to prevent delinquency cannot be measured by hours of service to individual clients, nor can their efforts be determined by following up individual clients or checking their court records at periodic intervals after treatment. Another difficulty is that the time frame for measuring effects of preventive services may be lengthy. For example, the ultimate effectiveness of programs that assist elementary school students to develop decision-making skills, in hopes of preventing drug abuse, may not be observable for several years.

If preventive services are to be maintained successfully, agencies must plan, implement, and operate them to achieve the desired effects without undesired results. Without evidence of effects, funding agencies are often reticent to provide resources for preventive services; administrators have difficulty knowing how to divide resources among preventive and treatment programs; and staff have few guides for orienting their preventive services for maximum effectiveness. Thus, it is important for the self-evaluating agency to develop methods for monitoring and evaluating their prevention activities.

The task of evaluating preventive services can be divided into three parts: (1) keeping track of the preventive services provided (monitoring prevention efforts); (2) determining outcomes and effects (assessing results of prevention

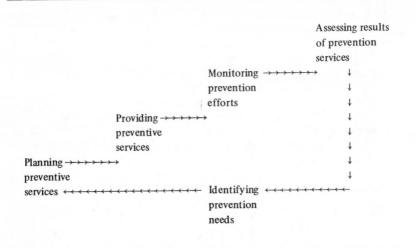

FIGURE 4.1   Cycle of Planning, Providing, and Evaluating Preventive Services in the Self-Evaluating Agency

services); and (3) planning or redesigning preventive services (identifying prevention needs). These three activities should be interrelated in a continuing cycle of assessment and improvement in the self-evaluating agency, as shown in Figure 4.1.

Case Example: "Prevention Services for Young Adults"

The preventive services of Shelton Heights Youth Services Center (SHYSC) serves as our case example with the following four service components: parent education, peer counseling, teacher training, and policy advocacy.

The Parenting Education Program. This program seeks to prevent problems such as delinquency and drug abuse by assisting parents in acquiring knowledge and skills for more effective parenting. The program's premise is that clear and open family communications and explicit responsibilities and rewards for children will decrease family problems which lead youth to engage in delinquency and drug abuse. The program consists of ten weekly workshops for parents which teach skills in communications, behavior management, and positive discipline using lectures, movies, role-playing, and group discussions.

The Peer Counseling Program. This program seeks to prevent behavior problems of violence and vandalism in the local high school by involving natural youth leaders in the school in a peer group counseling process. The program's premise is that peer influence can be mobilized to encourage development of favorable attitudes and commitment to school by providing students the opportunity and responsibility for resolving school problems. The program consists of leadership and student advisory groups. Leadership groups are composed of students nominated by school faculty as "positive" or "negative" leaders and invited to participate by program staff. The leadership groups meet for one school period each day to work to reduce misbehavior and attendance problems among members and to develop preventive strategies for disruptive behavior in the school. Student advisory groups, consisting of individual members of the leadership groups, work with other students with misbehavior, attendance, and other problems referred by teachers or students. The program is a collaborative effort of the school district and SHYSC.

The Teacher Training Project. Several staff members of SHYSC have developed a set of curriculum materials which focus on development of communication, decision-making, values clarification, and other "affective" skills. The package includes components from various affective education curricular used in drug abuse prevention programs. After testing the materials with junior high school students who were SHYSC clients, staff decided they would reach more students if the materials were integrated into the curricula of the local junior high schools. Subsequently, when teachers called from the school asking SHYSC to do a drug education course with their students, staff offered to train the teachers in use of the affective skills curriculum. Arrangements have been finalized with one of the local junior high school principals to provide a series of in-service teacher training workshops in the use of the materials.

School-Policy Advocacy Activities. SHYSC staff, in collaboration with the local chapter of the American Friends Service Committee (AFSC), reviewed local school district records and found that despite declining enrollments, the number of suspensions and dropouts had continually increased in the past five years. Further, they found that a disproportionate number of those who dropped out or were expelled were minority students. In recent months, SHYSC and the AFSC have been working with other community groups and individuals to encourage the school district to establish an alternative education program that would provide performance-based education, experiential learning, and counseling to students as an alternative to dropping out, suspension, or expulsion.

PLANNING FOR EFFORT MONITORING

Consultation and education services, interagency service coordination, or advocacy services are often undertaken in hopes of preventing problems before they develop. Agencies may identify several reasons to keep track of their efforts in these areas. For example, SHYSC needs to monitor its teacher training activities in order to show their board of directors and funding sources what they have done. Staff also want to monitor the time and resources spent in advocacy activities, as compared with other prevention efforts. Their advocacy work requires a great deal of time for attending meetings and talking on the phone. Monitoring this effort will provide realistic estimates of the resources required to plan and implement advocacy work.

You will recall that the decision-oriented evaluation model requires (1) clarifying the decisions that can be informed by information, (2) clarifying the specific information needed to inform the decisions, and (3) planning for the ultimate use of the information. The SHYSC director and staff identified the following questions to be answered by a monitoring system in their agency.

QUESTIONS TO BE ANSWERED BY A MONITORING SYSTEM

1. How much preventive service or activity do we produce?
2. How much of our preventive service time is spent in planning? How much time in service delivery?
3. How many people are we serving through our preventive services?
4. What groups or organizations are we serving or collaborating with in providing preventive services?
5. Are we doing what we planned and what we want to be doing in the preventive areas?

In addition to identifying specific questions, it is also important to determine how the information will be used. The SHYSC director identified the following specific uses for information to be produced by SHYSC's monitoring system.

SPECIFIC INFORMATION USES

1. Identification of the balance between preventive and treatment activities provided as a basis for planning program changes and reprioritizing efforts.
2. Identification of the time required for planning preventive services to allow for realistic planning and resource allocation for implementing preventive services.
3. Documentation of numbers of people reached through different preventive services to provide information for securing support for prevention program efforts and to inform planning.

4. Accounting for advocacy efforts and community education activities in order to market part of the preventive services of the agency.
5. Documentation of organizations and groups with which the agency works, to identify those which should be strongly supportive of the prevention program during times of political crises or when funds are needed, and to identify groups to cultivate because of their absence from the list.

Once the specific uses for information are clarified, it is important to involve appropriate board members and staff related to a specific program. Involvement in designing the system can produce three major benefits: (1) Clarifying the potential uses for the information should increase their investment in accurate information collecting, (2) gaining staff judgments about how information can best be obtained and recorded with minimal disruption to normal service activities, and (3) providing an opportunity to clarify service goals and priorities to develop a common base for long-term program planning. With these precautions in mind, the four-step decision-oriented program evaluation model can be used as a planning tool for developing an approach to evaluate the effort and effectiveness of SHYSC's advocacy project.

Principles to Remember. Take a break for a moment. Go back over what you've just read and jot down the principles that apply to your situation.

FOUR STEPS IN THE DECISION-ORIENTED
EVALUATION MODEL

Step 1: What is the problem and who cares?

The SHYSC's advocacy work with the AFSC is taking more time than the staff imagined it would. The agency has never kept track of the time spent on advocacy work in any systematic way. The administration realizes that the agency must limit its commitments to projects that can be completed without the staff "burning out."

The administrator is also concerned about funding for the advocacy effort. None of SHYSC's funds are specifically earmarked for that project. The administrator is involved in the advocacy work although his salary appears on SHYSC's records as administrative overhead, since he does not provide direct services to clients. He sees their advocacy work as prevention and would like to be able to keep track of it that way. He believes that recording advocacy work on the project will provide a basis for establishing a contract for funded advocacy work. SHYSC has two problems to write into Box 1 in Figure 4.2.

Clarifying the audience helps clarify the type of information needed. Identifying who cares about the problem allows determination of whether agency personnel are likely to use the information generated by a monitoring system when it becomes available. Why are they concerned? What do they want to do? This step involves determining how things would look if the problem was solved successfully. In this example, the SHYSC administrator wants to be able to do more realistic planning for advocacy activities and wants to be reimbursed for them.

What information is needed to solve the problem? In the SHYSC example, an accurate and complete record of the staff time spent planning and carrying out the advocacy project is needed (see Figure 4.2). The SHYSC information system will be based on staff activities rather than client activities.

Step 2: Where can we get the necessary information?

Information on staff time spent on different activities will come from staff themselves at SHYSC. How confidential is the needed information? In the SHYSC example confidentiality is not relevant. However, when collecting information on drug abuse, delinquency, or other personal data on clients, confidentiality is an issue that must be addressed in designing an information collection system.

We noted earlier that the people who have the least interest in collecting information are the very ones who are expected to collect it. The SHYSC administrator notes that John, who runs the peer counseling classes in the schools, and Bob, who has been doing the teacher training work, are both

(text continued on page 77)

Step 1: What is the problem and who cares?

1. What is the problem to be solved?	2. Who cares about the problem?	3. Why are they concerned? What do they want to do?	4. What information is needed to solve the problem?
1. a. We don't ever seem to plan for enough time for advocacy services. b. We haven't been able to get advocacy work funded.	Director and community service director.	a. Need to be able to do more realistic planning of time required for "advocacy" activities. b. Secure funding for advocacy activities.	Accurate record of time spent planning and carrying out advocacy projects.
2.			
3.			

FIGURE 4.2 Four-Step Guide for Determining, Assessing, and Meeting Information Needs

Step 2: Where can we get the necessary information?

5. Where could we get the information? Who will provide it?	6. How confidential is the needed information?	7. Who is likely to be least interested in providing needed information?	8. Why are they the least interested?	9. What resources will ensure its collection?
1. Keep track of staff time on different activities. Director. Staff. Board.	Not confidential.	Outreach staff (John, Bob).	They know how much time they spend recording. It takes extra time. Also may see it as threatening to record time spent "planning" with no tangible product	Must convince outreach staff of utility of information for planning and funding. Decrease their fears that it is to "check up" on them.
2.				
3.				

FIGURE 4.2 (continued)

Step 3: How good will the information be?			
10.	*11.*	*12.*	*13.*
How good will the information be?	What measures should be used?	What source documents/ collection instruments should be used or created?	How frequently will information be collected?
1. Good if Step 2 is successful.	Staff time recorded in quarter-hour increments. Develop *staff activity code.*	Staff activity form.	Daily (otherwise time estimates will be inaccurate).
2.			
3.			

FIGURE 4.2 (continued)

Step 4: Who will collect and report the information

14.	15.	16.	17.		
Who will collect and report the information?	How valid and reliable is the information likely to be?	How will information be fed back? (Format)	What is the utility of the information in solving the problem?		
1. Weekley: Turn in sheets at end of week to be summarized.	Not sure: Need to train staff in use of forms.	Total Advocacy Activities hours, Summary of staff activities. Summary sheet.	Assess after three months.		
2.					
3.					

FIGURE 4.2 (continued)

activists who hate record-keeping and paperwork because they see it as a waste of time.

Step 3: How good will the information be?

If the information generated by a monitoring system is to be used for program planning, it is important to find some incentive for people to record the information accurately. Ensuring the collection of the required information by mandating it as a job requirement probably will not guarantee good reporting, and may not provide information in which you have confidence. On the other hand, involving staff in planning for information collection, and thinking about how the information could be used to enhance services, may encourage more accurate forms completion. This is a benefit of using a collaborative planning process involving staff in developing the information system. The process can show that the administrator is interested in information primarily for planning purposes, rather than to monitor staff "compliance" with their job descriptions. Using these approaches to ensure collection of information should lead to greater confidence in its accuracy.

Frequently people fail to make a logical linkage between the problem to be solved and the measures used. In the SHYSC example the measure should be staff time broken down into standard intervals with some way to distinguish among different types of staff activities. The time intervals to be used to record staff activities must be decided. Time intervals small enough to pick up different activities, but not so small that they become a paperwork burden, are required. Categories of activities to be monitored also must be chosen. At SHYSC a decision is required as to whether to record only time spent on advocacy activities or time spent on a broader range of preventive services.

In the SHYSC case, keeping track of time spent on all prevention activities will have specific uses. Comparing time spent on the advocacy project against time spent on other prevention projects will help SHYSC make better decisions about pursuit of advocacy activities. If specific uses for the comprehensive information are identified and communicated, it is more likely that staff can be convinced of the value of a comprehensive system for monitoring their activities. Reviewing the uses for the information will also help in determining the specific categories of information needed. Because they want to assess the lead time and effort required to launch preventive services, SHYSC needs to separate planning from actual service delivery. Beyond this decision, they may choose to distinguish between direct services (such as the peer counseling groups and the parenting workshops), indirect services, and advocacy services (which include the school project we have been discussing). Alternately, they may choose to categorize by specific program component: teacher training, peer counseling, parenting workshops, advocacy projects, and a miscellaneous or a program development category for prevention services that are outside the four areas or are in preliminary planning stages.

What source documents/data collection instruments should be used or created? The time spent in prior steps should provide a basis for designing forms that will provide accurate and useful information. As the example has shown, designing an information system is a matter of thinking through the answers to a series of logical questions. At this point, the possibilities for using existing information sources should be explored before designing a new set of forms. In designing a monitoring system, a decision should also be made as to whether a staff activities accounting approach or a client-centered approach will provide the information needed.

Returning to the SHYSC example, a number of elements of the data collection instrument have already been identified. A separate accounting of time spent in each of the four prevention components is needed. It is also necessary to distinguish between planning time and time spent delivering services. The agency is also interested in documenting how many people are actually served in order to estimate the number of people reached through different prevention components. The administrator wants to know what other groups or organizations the agency is serving or collaborating with in providing preventive services. That information will be used for funding and to inform planning. The support of groups with which the agency has worked on the advocacy project can be enlisted in getting that component funded. The absence of particular organizations from the list of collaborating groups might suggest groups with which the agency should be working more closely. For example, SHYSC could collaborate with a number of community groups to increase participation in their parenting classes. A good record of the groups with which they are already working will allow them to identify gaps in their network of referral sources.

Using these items as the elements to be included in a staff activities form, the SHYSC administrator and her task force developed a draft form shown in Figure 4.3. They added the "Notes/Explanations" column so staff could elaborate on activities that fell under the "other" activity code, to allow for any explanations or elaborations staff wanted to provide (which could ultimately help in upgrading the form itself), and to make the form more immediately useful to staff who could use the column to jot down notes to themselves about new steps, problems encountered, and the like.

When and how frequently will data be collected? Staff activity information should be recorded as it happens if it is to be accurate. Given the amount of work involved in monitoring staff activity, it may be desirable to consider time sampling rather than asking staff to record information every day. Staff

Staff Name_____   Week of_____

Organization Contacted/ served	Prevention Activity	Planning Time	Service Time	Number Served	Notes and Explana- tions

PREVENTION
ACTIVITY CODES: TIME CODES:

1. Peer Counseling   1 = 15 minutes or less
2. Teacher Training   2 = 15-30 minutes
3. Parenting Training   3 = 30-45 minutes
4. School Advocacy   4 = 45 minutes to one hour, etc.
5. Other

FIGURE 4.3   SHYSC Prevention Services Staff Activities Form

can complete the form one week each month, or on a different designated day each week, to provide a sample of activities from which time estimates can be extrapolated. This should be discussed by the task force.

Step 4: Who will collect and report the information?

During the initiation of the system, it may be desirable for staff to turn in their activity forms on a weekly basis. Weekly submission allows more frequent monitoring to ensure that people are using the forms without difficulty. It also makes data summarization a smaller weekly task rather than a big job at the end of each month. Identify a place where forms will be turned in and establish a system to get back to people who have not turned in their form. Someone should be identified to summarize the information.

At SHYSC it was decided to review the results with staff at the end of each month as a basis for assessment and planning for the next month. The administration also suggested summarizing monthly reports each quarter to share with the board at the quarterly board meeting. She argued that such summaries would give the board a comprehensive picture of the agency's prevention programs that could help in involving them in considering the amount of work going on in the advocacy area and in planning to secure reimbursement for it.

How valid and reliable is the information likely to be? Once a form is developed and a plan has been established to collect the information, it is important to ask this question: "Is the information an accurate representation of what we decided we needed in Step 1 to solve our problem?" In other words, will the information collected accurately represent reality? Will some people provide higher time estimates than others even if they are engaged in the same activities? Will people use the same standards for completing their forms, so that activities can be compared across staff members and aggregated onto summary sheets with confidence? It is important to train staff in the use of the staff activities form if reliability is to be ensured.

How will the information be fed back (format) and how useful is it? At SHYSC, it was decided to show (1) the total hours spent on each prevention component in planning and service delivery, (2) a list of organizations worked with, and (3) total number of clients served. In addition, monthly summaries of activities by staff member were prepared to show how staff were dividing their time and to assist in planning for the next month.

Once the information collection system is in place and functioning, look at it periodically to see if it is really useful for solving the problem it was designed to address. Do not keep a system merely because it is in place. Schedule periodic reviews to decide if it is worth the resources it takes, whether it should be revised to be more useful, or whether it has fulfilled its purpose and can be dropped. Again, this step will be most useful if all the staff involved in the information system know it is coming and can be thinking about how to improve the information collection in order to make it less burdensome and more useful. Minimizing internal resistance to a new system helps to ensure the implementation of a system that is useful in agency decision making.

FORMS FOR MONITORING PREVENTIVE SERVICES

As shown in Chapter 3, the four-step process can be used to determine the content, format, and process of information collection to solve identified agency problems. Presented below are two additional examples of staff activity forms that might have been developed through such a process to keep track of preventive services.

Keeping track of prevention efforts by recording staff activity can provide information to be used for agency problem solving and planning and for funding. This section has suggested alternative recording systems that could be developed for these purposes.

PREVENTIVE SERVICES STAFF ACTIVITY FORM (Figure 4.4)

1. Content of the form.

This is a single form which keeps track of all prevention activities. It is completed by individual staff members for a specified period of time (such as a week). Information can be aggregated from individual staff forms and summarized at regular intervals for the entire agency or any program component. The form shows:

   a. How much time is spent in planning and delivering direct services (Columns 2 and 3), indrect services (Columns 5 and 6), and advocacy services (Columns 8 and 9). Time can be recorded in 15-minute increments.
   b. The number of people served directly (Column 4) and indirectly (Column 7).
   c. The principal organizations served or collaborating in the prevented services (Column 1).

2. Sample uses for information from staff activity form.

   a. A way to account for indirect and system advocacy activities as preventive services.
   b. A way of determining what indirect and advocacy services to pursue as part of prevention plans.
   c. A vehicle for documenting and comparing numbers served by different approaches
      – for planning and public relations.
      – for selection of prevention approaches.
   d. A vehicle for documenting time required for planning prevention services
      – for funding and accountability.
      – for realistic program planning.
   e. A means of identifying groups and organizations you work with
      – for identifying service gaps.
      – for identifying supportive organizations.
      – for funding documentation.

GOAL-FOCUSED STAFF ACTIVITY FORM (See Figure 4.4)

This is an alternative for use when prevention activities have been planned to address identified goals. This format allows assessment of prevention

PREVENTION SERVICES
STAFF ACTIVITY FORM

Staff Name _____   Week of _____

Organization Contacted	DIRECT SERVICES				INDIRECT SERVICES				ADVOCACY	
	Planning Time	Service Delivery		Planning Time	Service Delivery		Planning Time	Activity
		Time	# Served		Time	# Served		
COL. 1	COL. 2	COL. 3	COL. 4	COL. 5	COL. 6	COL. 7	COL. 8	COL. 9

PREVENTION SERVICES
GOAL-FOCUSED ACTIVITY FORM

ORGANIZATION CONTACTED	TYPE OF CONTACT*	GOAL 1: To increase work opportunities for youth		GOAL 2: To increase abilities of community members to cope with stress		GOAL 3: Development Activities
		Time	# Served	Time	# Served	Time

*CONTACT CODE

1 = Direct Service
2 = Provide consultation (indirect services)
3 = Provide training (indirect services)
4 = Receive consultation
5 = Receive training
6 = Advocacy activity
7 = Planning, general information, sharing contact
8 = In-house planning or preparation

FIGURE 4.4 Staff Activity and Goal-Focused Activity Forms

activities in the context of a prevention plan and allows assessment of the extent of which prevention activities are oriented to goals of the agency's prevention plan.

CONCLUSION

The aim of this chapter has been to demonstrate the use of the four-step model in assessing the factors involved in measuring effort enroute to evaluating effectiveness. The steps include:

1. What is the problem and who cares?
2. Where can we get the necessary information?
3. How good will the information be?
4. Who will collect and report the information?

Some of the unique difficulties raised by measuring effort related to prevention services were discussed. Specific suggestions for planning the information collection process are provided as a foundation for using the four-step model to monitor effort in a youth advocacy program. In addition, alternative data recording methods were described. In the next chapter we will focus less on effort and more on evaluating program effectiveness.

REFERENCES

EMPEY, L. T. (1978) American Delinquency: Its Meaning and Construction. Homewood, IL: Dorsey.

HIRSCHI, T., M. J. HINDELANG, and J. WEIS (1979) "The status of self-report measures," in M. W. Klein and K. S. Teilman (eds.) Handbook of Criminal Justice Evaluation. Beverly Hills, CA: Sage.

SKOK, J. A. (1978) Evaluation of the Pennsylvania Youth Services System Project. Wilkes-Barre: Center for the Study of Delinquency, Pennsylvania Department of Education, Wilkes College.

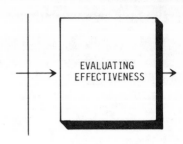

Chapter 5

EVALUATING PROGRAM EFFECTIVENESS

In this chapter we continue to look at prevention services but with an emphasis on evaluating program effectiveness. While Chapter 4 described the monitoring of the amounts and kinds of prevention activities related to program effort, this chapter describes different ways of assessing program effectiveness in such prevention programs as a parenting workshop and a teacher training class. These diverse examples serve to illustrate how question-naires, records, or documents can be used as data collection strategies to measure results. In assessing the results of prevention efforts, the staff of a self-evaluating agency should consider (1) counting changes versus measuring effectiveness, (2) lag time in measuring outcome, and (3) measuring the ultimate impact on clients. You may want to review the selected evaluation principles and practices noted in Appendix B as an aid in understanding the evaluation process to be described in this chapter.

EVALUATING EFFECTIVENESS VERSUS IMPACT

Perhaps the most important question about any social program is, "Did it work?" Did our peer counseling program reduce violence and vandalism in the school? Did the teacher training project reduce drug abuse among students? These are questions of program effectiveness. The most rigorous evaluation of program effectiveness usually requires an experimental design by which it can be determined that the interventions caused the observed results. However, experimental designs involve complex technical and ethical problems that are often difficult for the self-evaluating agency to overcome.

Fortunately, a closely related question can be answered much more easily. This is the question of what happened to persons or conditions that were targeted by a program. For example, was there less drug use among students in the classes of teachers trained in affective education approaches? This type of information has been called impact or outcome enumeration, which tells us whether things got worse or better after the program was initiated (Lofquist, 1979). It does not prove that the program was responsible for the results. Nevertheless, determining whether things are better or worse can provide very useful information for the self-evaluating agency. Several of the evaluation approaches described below are outcome enumerations. These techniques for gathering information *cannot* prove that the program was responsible for the observed results.

A difficulty in assessing results of prevention efforts is created by the fact that the desired results may not be observable for some time. As an example, consider a training program in affective skills offered to third- and fourth-grade teachers as a drug abuse prevention strategy. Students of these teachers might not be expected to use psychoactive drugs, even if not exposed to the program, for five years or more. The self-evaluating agency probably will not have the resources to follow these students over a long period to measure their drug use.

Two implications are important. First, even without assessing the ultimate outcome of student drug use, other intermediate outcomes can be assessed. Did teachers learn the techniques presented? Did teachers use these techniques in their classes? Even without long-term outcome data, answers to these questions can indicate how the teacher training program can be improved. Second, when long-term outcomes cannot be assessed by the agency, it becomes important to select prevention techniques that have either a strong conceptual foundation or have been shown by research to be promising or effective in achieving their goals. It is not sufficient for the agency which seeks to launch an effective prevention program simply to offer those services with which staff are familiar or comfortable, and to assume optimistically that they will result in effective prevention.

Prevention interventions, no matter how well intended, are never guaranteed success. In some instances they may even do more harm than good. For example, many early drug abuse prevention efforts relied on a drug information approach. Young people were taught about the risks and effects of various drugs in hopes that this would facilitate wiser decisions about drug use. Follow-up evaluations showed that the effect of these efforts was to increase curiosity and experimental drug use among students. When your agency is unable to assess fully the effects of its prevention program, it is important to search for and use preventive approaches that have been evaluated and show promise.

The fact that prevention efforts may not identify individuals clearly as service recipients can also make it difficult to assess the results of prevention activities. Indirect services, such as teacher training or advocacy efforts designed to develop alternatives to school suspensions, may seek to prevent drug abuse or violence among students. However, since students are not directly served, it becomes more difficult to use information about those served to discover program results. Information collection designs that assess intervening results, rather than ultimate effectiveness, as well as designs that look at aggregated measures across an institution (such as rates of violence in a school), can be used to overcome this problem.

DESIGN FOR ASSESSING PREVENTION RESULTS

This section includes two designs for assessing results of prevention programs. The designs are presented in order of increasing difficulty and rigor. The first design is a posttest design for assessing client satisfaction during or after program participation. It is relatively simple to conduct and is useful and fairly typical for educational, training, or counseling programs. It is an outcome enumeration design that allows an agency to determine whether those served are satisfied with the services and how they think services could be improved. The design does not allow determination of program effectiveness in changing behavior, knowledge, or attitudes.

The second design is a pre-post-test design that compares the knowledge, attitudes, and self-reported behaviors of an unserved group with those people who received program services. This is a simple quasi-experimental design allowing greater confidence that observed results are related to program services. It is presented in the section on documenting differences in knowledge, attitudes, or behaviors.

The prevention programs of SHYSC are used to illustrate the two designs. Before studying the designs, review the six steps of the objectives-oriented approach to program evaluation noted in Chapter 3 and the selected evaluation principles and practices described in Appendix B. An example of the objectives-oriented approach to evaluating the parenting workshop program is noted in Figure 5.1.

DOCUMENTING CLIENT SATISFACTION:
THE PARENTING WORKSHOP

SHYSC has offered several parenting workshop series. They have used a simple attendance sheet to monitor participation and have found that only about 60 percent of the parents who come the first week complete the ten-week series. By the end of the fourth week, approximately 30 percent stop attending. The director and her staff are interested in increasing the proportion of people who complete the program. They agree that knowledge

Step 1: SHYSC's Mission

As a youth serving agency supported primarily by the local United Way, SHYSC has the mission of meeting the social and emotional needs of youth up to the age of 21 and their families. The service approaches used to accomplish this mission include individual and family counseling, youth advocacy, youth education and recreation, and *public education and information for lay and professional groups.* The desired results of these services include improved skills in managing communication, developmental, and educational needs of youth in the Shelton Heights community.

Step 2: Program Goals

Parenting Workshop Series: 1) Provision of a series of six weekly evening sessions on relevant parenting knowledge and skills, 2) in an informal atmosphere of fifteen to twenty parents, 3) staffed by a male and female workshop leader, and 4) at a reasonable fee which covers half the cost of the workshop series. The desired impact of the workshops include: 1) increased parent knowledge and skill related to parenting, 2) reduced demand for individual and family counseling on the part of workshop participants, and 3) increased capacity to handle the problems experienced by their children in the areas of communication, education, and developmental growth.

Step 3: Program Objectives

Impact objectives related to relevant knowledge and skills: 1) Family member roles and responsibilities, 2) communication skills, 3) shared decision-making techniques, and 4) handling family conflict.

Process objectives related to the delivery of the workshops: 1) Informal atmosphere, 2) leadership of workshop facilitators, 3) appropriateness of fees, and 4) use of teaching methods including lectures, demonstrations, role playing, discussion, and handout materials.

Step 4: Measuring the Impact and Process Objectives

Type of Measures: 1) Written consumer satisfaction questionnaires, 2) debriefing sessions at the end of each evening, 3) telephone follow-up surveys after the workshop series, and 4) indicators of calls from participants for individual and family counseling.

Frequency of Measures: 1) End of each session, 2) middle of series and at the end, 3) three months after the series, and 4) one year after series.

Step 5: Measuring the Participant's Objectives

Participant Objectives: Degree to which each participant is assisted in specifying, monitoring, and assessing personal objectives related to workshop participation.

Frequency of Progress Checks: 1) Each session, 2) middle of series and at the end, or 3) through rigorous follow-up and monitoring for three months after the workshop series.   *(continued)*

FIGURE 5.1   Using the Objective-Oriented Model for Evaluating Parenting Workshops

Step 6: Using the Results

> *Major Areas of Interest:* 1) Teaching methods, 2) subject matter, and 3) changes at home.
>
> *Organization of Findings:* 1) Anticipated internal factors, 2) unanticipated internal factors, 3) anticipated external factors, and 4) unanticipated external factors.
>
> *Modifying Workshops:* 1) Process objectives and methods, and 2) impact objectives and methods.
>
> *Presentation of Findings:* 1) Participants, 2) staff, and 3) board members.

FIGURE 5.1 (continued)

of why people drop out would indicate whether the problem was related to content and format of the workshops. They realize that in order to determine why people drop out, they would need to follow up on people who had stopped attending. The information sought would be somewhat confidential, so they would need to collect it in a way that would guarantee anonymity to people surveyed. They think this would increase the honesty of people's answers.

They conclude that people who have dropped out of the program might not be very interested in responding to such a survey unless the program could offer some incentive. Dropouts might be unhappy with the program, might have dropped out for private personal reasons, or might feel guilty about dropping out. They agree that they have no resources to ensure that people will respond to the survey, beyond the promise that honest answers could help improve the program. They are concerned that given such limited resources to ensure collection, they would probably not get responses from many of the dropouts, even if they could assure them anonymity.

They realize that doing such a survey would require either a mailed questionnaire or follow-up interviews with dropouts by phone or in person. They decide that they do not have the staff resources to do phone or in-person follow-ups. Anonymous mailed questionnaires would probably get few responses from dropouts and may not provide a valid representation of the views of the entire group. Therefore, they pause to reflect on alternative types and sources of information that could help them increase the proportion of people who complete the program.

This time, staff agree that asking participants to evaluate the workshops at the end of each session might provide information useful for solving the attrition problem. They hope to determine how useful the workshops have been by learning (1) what participants thought were the most and least valuable teaching approaches and subjects covered, (2) whether participants have applied any of the parenting approaches in their own parenting, and (3) whether participants have found that these applications resulted in better relationships in the family. This information might also provide clues for redesigning the course in order to increase its immediate utility to participants. If the program can be made useful to participants, the number of dropouts may decrease.

This new approach requires an anonymous survey to ensure that participants answer honestly. But this survey should provide information in which staff have greater confidence. If participants are asked to complete a brief questionnaire at the end of each session, whose purpose is to help improve the workshop's utility, participants should see value in participating in the survey. Staff are more confident that this information collection approach will get responses from a good proportion of participants, even if they subsequently fail to show up for other sessions. They decide that this approach will provide a relatively complete and valid picture of the views of both dropouts and program completers.

The staff discuss the possible measures to be used on the questionnaire. They want participants to evaluate the utility of teaching approaches and subjects covered in the workshops, to identify how they have used the course content at home, and to identify any results of their efforts at home. After the discussion, the two staff members who lead the parenting workshops agree to draft a questionnaire, with the help of the agency's evaluation consultant, that will tape these issues. They agree to bring back the draft questionnaire to the rest of the group for review in two weeks.

At the next planning session, the draft questionnaire is reviewed by staff and finalized (Figure 5.2 provides an example of the Consumer Satisfaction Survey). Staff decide that it will be most useful to review and summarize the questionnaire information after each workshop so that it will not become a mass of information no one would want to handle. The workshop leaders are eager to see the information, so they agree to work with a student intern placed at the agency to summarize the information each week. Results are to be reported monthly to the rest of the staff so that they can offer suggestions for use of the information. These reports are to be both written and oral. The workshop leaders and student intern will summarize monthly results on a blank questionnaire, indicating frequencies and percentages of responses and also showing illustrative comments by participants. They will then review these orally with staff and discuss implications and possible solutions to problems uncovered. Staff agree that using an anonymous questionnaire and sampling 100 percent of the workshop participants will probably provide valid and reliable information.

Program Evaluation Form*

To make the parenting workshops most effective, we need your help. Please answer the following questions candidly. Your answers will be strictly confidential. You need not identify yourself on this sheet. Your honest answers will help us improve the program.

1. WHAT IS YOUR REACTION TO THE COURSE SO FAR?

_____Very pleased   _____Somewhat disappointed   _____Not sure yet

_____Somewhat pleased   _____Very disappointed

Comments? _____

_____

_____

2. PLEASE RATE THE TEACHING METHODS USED SO FAR

	Not very useful	Somewhat useful	Very useful	Not sure yet
a. Lectures (check one)	_____	_____	_____	_____
b. Demonstrations of techniques	_____	_____	_____	_____
c. Role-playing (check one)	_____	_____	_____	_____
d. Discussion (check one)	_____	_____	_____	_____
e. Handout materials (check one)	_____	_____	_____	_____

Please make any suggestions you have for improving the course methods based on your experience so far.

_____

_____

_____

_____

3. PLEASE RATE THE SUBJECT MATTER COVERED SO FAR.

	Not very useful	Somewhat useful	Very useful	Not sure yet
a. Roles and responsibilities of family members	_____	_____	_____	_____
b. Communication skills	_____	_____	_____	_____
c. Shared decision-making techniques	_____	_____	_____	_____
d. Handling family conflict	_____	_____	_____	_____

Which skill do you feel you are *using most effectively* so far? Describe!

_____

_____

_____

_____

FIGURE 5.2   Parenting Workshop Consumer Satisfaction Survey

Which skill do you find *most difficult to apply* so far? Describe!

_____

_____

_____

_____

4. HAVE YOU SEEN ACTUAL POSITIVE CHANGES AT HOME IN THE
   FOLLOWING AREAS SINCE YOU STARTED THE PROGRAM?

		Not yet	*Some positive change*	*Much positive change*
a.	Less frequent family conflicts?	_____	_____	_____
b.	Less intense family conflicts?	_____	_____	_____
c.	More cooperation among family members?	_____	_____	_____
d.	More mutual respect shown among family members?	_____	_____	_____
e.	Clearer communication among family members?	_____	_____	_____
f.	Responsibilities for tasks clearly divided among family members?	_____	_____	_____
g.	Children assume greater responsibility for decisions and their consequences?	_____	_____	_____
h.	Others? Please describe!	_____	_____	_____

_____

_____

_____

_____

Have things gotten worse in any of the above areas? _____Yes _____No

If so, please describe! _____

_____

_____

_____

Any other comments or suggestions? _____

_____

_____

_____

*Some items adapted from effectiveness Training, Solana Beach, California, and from Family Education Center, Santa Rosa, California

FIGURE 5.2 (continued)

TABLE 5.1   Parenting Workshop Consumer Satisfaction Survey
Results — Week 4 (percentages)

TEACHING METHODS	Not Useful	Somewhat Useful	Very Useful	Not Sure
Lectures	0	65	30	5
Demonstrations	0	30	70	0
Role-play	0	20	80	0
Discussions	0	50	40	10
Handouts	10	70	10	10
SUBJECT MATTER				
Family responsibilities	0	42	58	0
Communication	0	26	74	0
Decision-making	0	42	58	0
Conflict resolution	0	40	50	10

CHANGES AT HOME	Not Yet	Some Change	Much Change
Frequency of conflict	72%	28%	0
Intensity of conflict	63%	27%	10%
Cooperation	55%	40%	5%
Mutual respect	60%	28%	12%
Communication	30%	60%	10%
Division of responsibilities	55%	40%	5%
Children more responsible	75%	25%	0

RESULTS

After one month the staff met to review the Consumer Satisfaction results from the first four weeks of information collection. In reviewing the summary questionnaires in preparation for the meeting, workshop leaders found some results they thought were particularly interesting. Table 5.1 highlights these results for the fourth week of the parenting workshop.

While it appeared that participants were generally satisfied with subject matter and teaching methods, workshop leaders were concerned about the percentage of participants who indicated they had not yet seen changes at home. They feared that parents who did not see results at home might drop out because they were not finding the workshop helpful in resolving family problems. They reviewed these parents' comments and noticed that many had failed to comment on either the skills they were using most effectively or the skills they found most difficult to apply. Some of the comments that did appear seemed rather general: "I'm trying to use all the things we've learned here as problems come up at home," or "It's sometimes hard to remember to do what I've learned in the workshop, especially in the heat of battle at home."

As staff discussed these results, they brainstormed approaches that might increase the likelihood of changes at home. They decided that homework assignments for practicing each of the skills might be helpful. At the end of each workshop session, parents could decide on a specific way they would practice the skill learned during the next week. Parents would contract with themselves to use the skill in a particular way. Parents would be asked at the beginning of the next workshop session to discuss their attempt to use the skill and what had happened as a result. Staff agreed that this procedure might encourage parents to begin practicing specific skills at home and that this, in turn, might result in more obvious improvement at home. On the other hand, some staff said that the homework assignments might be threatening to some parents and that they might decide not to come to the following week's workshop if they had not done the homework assignment. The homework assignment could have the opposite effect on attendance than that intended.

Workshop leaders decided to go ahead with the homework assignments, but to try to assess this possible problem by adding an item to the teaching methods section of the Program Evaluation Form on "Homework Assignments." In this way, they could see if participants considered the assignments useful or not.

Once the homework assignments were instituted, more parents began to report changes at home on the program evaluation forms, and the dropout rate fell to 10 percent. The director of SHYSC saw the value of the consumer satisfaction surveys for funding and accountability. She began to share results quarterly with her board of directors and used them in preparing a refunding application to the Drug Abuse Commission.

SUMMARY

Consumer satisfaction surveys represent one of the simplest forms of outcome evaluation. They cannot prove whether prevention services are effective. However, they can answer the following questions:

1. Are those served satisfied with the services?
2. Do they perceive the services as useful?
3. Do they think that the services have helped make things better?
4. How do consumers think the services could be improved to be more effective?

Even where specific improvements are not directly suggested by consumers, their responses to a survey can indicate areas that should be upgraded, as illustrated above. Consumer satisfaction surveys can be useful any time direct or indirect services are offered. At SHYSC, for example, such surveys could also be used in the peer counseling and teacher training programs.

Consumer satisfaction surveys have the advantage of being relatively unthreatening to clients, since they explicitly seek clients' evaluations of the services and do not directly measure changes in clients' attitudes, knowledge, or behavior. However, for this very reason they do not provide accurate indications of actual program effects. They do not directly measure whether things got better before or after the program, but rely on the judgments of clients and consumers for this information. These judgments can be biased by a number of factors. In fact, consumers generally indicate more favorable results than can be documented by more rigorous evaluation methods. Therefore, results of consumer satisfaction surveys should *not* be used to try to show that a program actually changed behavior, knowledge, or attitudes. Despite this limitation, consumer satisfaction surveys can be useful whenever direct or indirect services are offered.

DOCUMENTING DIFFERENCES IN KNOWLEDGE, ATTITUDES, OR BEHAVIORS

SHYSC staff believe that training junior high teachers in using affective education methods is a promising approach for drug abuse prevention. However, they continue to receive requests to conduct drug information classes in junior high schools. They would like to discontinue the drug information classes and to concentrate on teacher training for several reasons. First, they think they can have a broader impact on a larger number of young people if they train teachers. The small staff of SHYSC can work directly with only one class of students at a time. In the same amount of time, they could be training a group of teachers to use their new skills with several classes of students. Further, the teachers have prolonged contact with students, while SHYSC staff can work with students for only a limited time. Finally, SHYSC staff are aware that drug information approaches used alone may be associated with increased student use of drugs (Grizzle, 1970; Stuart, 1974). They think that teaching decision making and other skills may hold greater promise for helping students to decide against drug abuse (Schaps et al., 1978; Slimmon, 1973; Williams et al., 1968).

Currently, the agency faces a dilemma. School personnel who want the SHYSC drug information classes to continue are pressuring staff to provide this service. One junior high vice principal said he thinks SHYSC is becoming less responsive to his school's needs. He does not think teachers in his school should participate in the teacher training program. He does not see what affective education has to do with student drug use. He has also privately told the SHYSC staff that teachers in his school would not use the affective education curriculum even if they received training.

SHYSC staff decide to use the four-step decision-oriented model to see how evaluation might help them solve their problem. They meet to discuss the resistance of several of the community's junior high schools to participate in the teacher training program. They would like to secure broader school participation in the teacher training program, which would allow a more efficient use of staff resources than continuing to offer drug information classes directly to students. It would provide additional revenues to SHYSC in the form of in-service training funds from schools and, staff hope, lead to more effective drug abuse prevention.

In their discussions, staff identify two general points in the arguments of the critics of teacher training. First is the charge that teachers will not use the affective skills in their classes. Staff agree that this could, in fact, be a problem with the teacher training approach. If teachers did not use the new methods, the approach would not have much chance of being effective. Second is the issue of whether affective skills, combined with drug information, do change students' attitudes toward drugs and drug use. From this discussion, staff decide to answer three questions:

   a. Do teachers who receive the training learn the skills and develop knowledge about alcohol and drugs presented in the training program?
   b. Do teachers who receive the training use the skills in their classes?
   c. Do students in the classes of trained teachers change their attitudes toward drug use or drug-using behaviors? Do they develop better decision-making, problem-solving, and coping skills?

Staff conclude that to answer all three questions they would need to collect information from teachers who participate in the workshops, and from students in their classes, as well as from students in classes where SHYSC staff present drug information sessions. Currently, the workshops are being offered in only one junior high in the district. The drug information classes are usually presented in other schools that have not agreed to participate in the teacher training project. Staff are concerned that comparing students in the teacher training condition in one school with students in the drug information condition in another would introduce many sources of bias. There might be very different attitudes and patterns of drug use in the different schools. The very fact that the administration in one school is supportive of the teacher training approach sets that school apart from other junior high schools in the district. Staff want the research to stand up to criticism from those who oppose teacher training workshops. They would like to minimize the chance that people will dismiss it if it is favorable to that approach. They would also like to be able to pursue the most effective of the two prevention strategies based on the information they collect.

Staff discuss the possibility of using an experimental design to compare the teacher training and direct drug information approaches. If they could work in a single school and randomly assign teachers to the workshops, while providing drug information sessions in classes of teachers not randomly assigned to the workshops, they could compare the effectiveness of the two approaches. But they know that teachers and the administration of the junior high currently participating in the teacher training program would oppose the idea of withholding the workshops from some teachers who wanted them. As they discuss this dilemma, they consider a possible solution. They have scheduled workshops for groups of six to ten teachers. Perhaps they could simply use classes of teachers scheduled for later workshops as the control group. Only random assignment to early or later workshop sessions would be required. Those teachers assigned to the current sessions would be the experimental group and those assigned to later sessions would be controls. To compare the two prevention approaches, using this experimental design, SHYSC staff would have to present drug information sessions to students in the classes of the controls.

Although staff would like to pursue this experimental approach, they recognize some problems. First, there are not enough staff to do both the teacher training workshops and the drug information sessions. Second, their contract calls for conducting two sets of teacher training workshops per semester in the participating school, so that all participating teachers are trained by the end of the school year. Staff recognize that even with random assignment of teachers to training sessions, they would not have a very long follow-up period to assess and compare actual student drug use before the control teachers got trained. Staff reconsider their plan. They realize that with the limited resources they have available they will have to use a less ambitious design. They decide to drop the idea of comparing the teacher training program and the direct drug information approach. They know that rigorous studies of the effectiveness of drug information approaches have already shown them to be ineffective for drug abuse prevention. They decide to use this information as evidence for the lack of effectiveness of that approach. They will focus their evaluation efforts on their teacher training workshops and not try to offer alcohol and drug information sessions to students in classes of teachers in the control group. However, they want to maintain a design that will allow them to assess the effectiveness of the teacher training program in changing students' knowledge, attitudes, and use of drugs. They decide to revise their third question: "Is the teacher training program effective in changing student knowledge, attitudes, and use of alcohol and drugs?" Outlined below is the design the staff then develop for answering their three questions:

   a. Do teachers who receive the training learn the skills and develop the knowledge about alcohol and drugs presented in the training program?

To assess this, half the participating teachers (selected randomly) in each workshop are asked to complete a pretest at the beginning of the first workshop session; the other half are asked to complete the same test as a posttest at the end of the final workshop. This pre-post design allows staff to assess whether teachers had the requisite skills and knowledge to implement the affect education drug abuse prevention curriculum in their classes before and after being trained in its use. Each teacher completes the questionnaire only once, so there is no problem of testing effects, little likelihood of teacher resistance to completing the same questionnaire twice, and no problem of selection effects.

Staff decide to aggregate all pretest scores from all workshops during the year as the measure of teachers' skills and knowledge before workshop participation. They will use these results as a baseline for comparison with aggregated posttest scores. They recognize that some of the pretest scores of teachers who participate in the workshop at the end of the year may be affected by interaction with colleagues who participated in the earlier workshops. However, they decide that this will only serve to make the comparison a more rigorous test of the workshops. They conclude that the approach will generate a large enough number of pretests and posttests (approximately 20 each) to allow for simple statistical comparisons of the mean scores of untrained and trained teachers.

Since teachers will be assigned randomly to receive either pretests or posttests, the possibility that characteristics of individual teachers with greatly biased results will be minimized. For assessing effects of the workshops on teachers, this design is only slightly better than a one-group, pretest-posttest design (Campbell and Stanley, 1963). Its advantages are that teachers have to take the test only once, thus minimizing testing effects. Additionally, the fact that both pretest and posttest scores are obtained throughout the year helps to control for other "historical" events in the school which could have influenced teacher knowledge and skills. While staff would like to give pretests and posttests to a separate sample of teachers who are not participating in the workshops at all (a nonequivalent control group), they decide that they do not have the resources to recruit and test teachers outside the workshops.

Rather than design totally new instruments for these tests, staff contact their state agency to find out about instruments that might be available from other teacher training workshops. They find an instrument developed for assessing teacher knowledge about alcohol and its effects; attitudes toward alcohol use, and its regulation; discussion-leading abilities; and decision-making or problem-solving skills. Staff revise this instrument to fit their own needs. (Figure 5.3 shows sample items from the questionnaire which illustrate various question formats.) Since some of the items on the questionnaire ask teachers' attitudes toward certain behavior, staff agree that privacy and confidentiality should be protected. They use anonymous questionnaires, since they do not plan to match individual questionnaires for any purpose.

b. Do teachers who receive the training use the skills in their classes?

To assess use of the curriculum in teachers' classrooms, staff develop a consumer satisfaction survey which they send to each participating teacher two months after the teacher completes the workshop. In addition to questions about the adequacy of the workshops, the questionnaire asks teachers (1) about specific uses of the workshop materials and drug abuse curriculum, (2) to estimate number of classroom hours spent in using the curriculum in specific classroom activities, and (3) about their confidence in teaching drug abuse prevention to students since attending the workshops. Again, the questionnaires are anonymous. Though staff recognize that self-reports by teachers regarding use of the materials and curriculum provide less valid measures than direct observations of classrooms, they are willing to accept this measure. Since they do not have enough resources to conduct direct observations of teachers, they hope that the anonymity guaranteed teachers will encourage honest responses, and they design the questions as evaluations of the workshops rather than as evaluations of the teachers to minimize the chance they will be "threatening" to teachers.

Staff are concerned that some teachers might not return the anonymous questionnaires. They reason that the teachers least likely to respond might be those who have not used the workshop curriculum, thus biasing results. Therefore, they send a card with each questionnaire and ask the teacher to print his or her name on the card and to return the card separately when returning the anonymous questionnaire. After two weeks, staff follow up with teachers who have not sent in cards and personally ask them to complete and turn in their questionnaires. Using this method, they receive questionnaires from 34 (or 85 percent) of the 40 participating teachers.

c. Do students in classes of trained teachers change their attitudes toward drug use or drug-using behavior?

Staff are most interested in assessing changes in students' decision-making and coping abilities and their knowledge of, attitudes toward, and use of alcohol and drugs after exposure to the drug abuse prevention curriculum.

INTRODUCTION: Evaluation is an integral part of any successful training enterprise, and the training you recently had in the subject of alcohol and alcoholism needs to be evaluated. PLEASE NOTE that it is the *training* that is being evaluated here, not yourself. This set of questionnaires is just one of a number of measures by which some judgments can be made about the effectiveness of the training program, but it is vital that everyone participate in the evaluation who has participated in the training, so your cooperation in filling out the questionnaire will be deeply appreciated. Your anonymity is guaranteed by the evaluators. Neither your name nor any of the questionnaires themselves will be made available to school personnel or even to the training directors. All data will be reported in the form of statistical tabulations only. Please do your best to answer every question. Most can be answered simply by circling a number, but in a few cases you will be asked to write out your own answer to a question. Feel free to write any of your own comments or questions in the margins or on the backs of the pages.

PART ONE: Knowledge About Alcohol and Alcoholism

INSTRUCTIONS: This first questionnaire requires that you merely circle the number of the answer you think best for each question.

Behavioral Effects of Alcohol

A. The body function that would first become impaired by drinking alcoholic beverages is:

1. Judgment and coordination.
2. Muscular coordination.
3. Sense of hearing.
4. Sense of balance.
5. Sense of vision.

B. A combination of alcohol and barbiturates, when ingested, has what kind of effect on the central nervous system?

1. Additive.
2. Potentiative or synergistic.
3. In combination, the two drugs neutralize each other.
4. Inhibitive.
5. In combination, the two drugs stimulate the nervous system.

C. Most experts believe that:

1. There is no known cure for alcoholism.
2. Alcoholism is an untreatable illness.
3. Alcoholism is a treatable illness.
4. Alcoholism can be cured through chemical means.
5. 1 and 3.

(continued)

FIGURE 5.3   Sample Items from Teacher Training Questionnaire*

D. For each hypothetical situation described below, please circle the number at the right that best describes your feelings about it.

	Approve	*Neutral*	*Disapprove*
1. Parents who serve alcoholic beverages to their own teenagers at home.	1	2	3
2. High school students who hold beer parties or "keggers."	1	2	3
3. A hostess who shows her hospitality by continually urging more alcohol on her guests.	1	2	3
4. A host at a party who lets a heavily drinking guest drive home, after being assured by the guest that he is able to do so safely.	1	2	3
5. A colleague who abstains totally from drinking on religious principles.	1	2	3

E. The following statements about the use and/or regulation of alcohol are matters of opinion or policy preference, with no one "right" answer. Circle the number in each case which indicates your agreement with the statement.

	Approve	*Neutral*	*Disapprove*
1. The schools must provide education about alcohol use and abuse in an effort to prevent or reduce alcoholism.	1	2	3
2. Whether or not to drink on a certain occasion is strictly an individual decision, in which other people should not interfere.	1	2	3
• 3. It is a teacher's responsibility to make sure that his/her students appreciate the dangers involved in starting to drink.	1	2	3
4. Occasional drinking for relaxation is a perfectly acceptable use of alcohol.	1	2	3

FIGURE 5.3 (continued)

F. There is much discussion lately about "responsible" and "irresponsible" drinking. For the situations described below, circle your interpretation of the behaviors which seem to you responsible and/or irresponsible.

   1. A father, overhearing his son's plan to join with others at a beer party the night of high school graduation, decides to offer his own home to the son and friends for the party, so he can keep an eye on them. Knowing that they could obtain beer from somewhere anyway, the father agrees to buy the beer for the party, on the strict promise by the son that no beer will be served to anyone younger than those in the graduating class.

	Responsible	Irresponsible	Not Sure
What is your interpretation of the father's behavior?	1	2	3
What is your interpretation of the son's promise to his father?	1	2	3

PART TWO: Leading Discussions

INSTRUCTIONS: This part of the questionnaire deals with techniques of leading discussions under the various circumstances that a teacher might face. The first section asks you simply to match several techniques with a corresponding number of possible situations. In the second section, you will be presented with some actual or hypothetical scenarios and asked to write down the procedure(s) you might follow in such circumstances.

SECTION A: From the list at the right, choose the technique that you think *best* fits the situation indicated at the left. Write the *number* of that technique (Nos. 1 through 6) in the space provided.

Situation

_____1. If you want to begin a class discussion . . .

_____2. If you do not understand what a student said . . .

_____3. If a student begins verbally attacking another student . . .

_____4. If the class is silent in response to your question . . .

_____5. If a student is asking for specific information . . .

_____6. If a student makes a comment relevant to the subject being discussed, and you understand . . .

Technique

a. focus-setting

b. structuring

c. clarifying

d. teacher silence

e. responding to student's data gathering

f. acknowledging

(continued)

FIGURE 5.3 (continued)

SECTION B: Next, four situations are posed that might arise in classroom discussion groups. How would you as the discussion facilitator respond to these situations? After each paragraph you will find a space to write down what you would say or do if you were confronted with these situations in your own classroom. There are many appropriate responses. Write down what you would actually say. You will probably have certain reasons for saying what you do, but this questionnaire is designed to find out only WHAT YOU WOULD SAY and *not* WHY you would say it.

1. After viewing a film with your class covering such things as the long-term physical effects of alcohol, accidents caused by drinking drivers, and days of work missed due to alcoholism, the class has been discussing some of the problems caused by heavy alcohol use. After about 20 minutes of discussion, one student turns to you and says, "You may say that drinking is so bad, but don't you drink?" What would you say?

_____

_____

_____

_____

_____

_____

_____

*Items are from the "Here's Looking At You!" Project (Educational Service District 121, Seattle, Washington, and Washington State University, Pullman, Washington)

FIGURE 5.3 (continued)

They know that the extent to which teachers use the approaches taught in the training workshops will influence the possible effects on students. They consider trying to link teacher and student questionnaires to explore this possibility. However, concluding that this would be too complex and would also prevent the use of anonymous questionnaires for assessing teachers' use of the curriculum materials, they decide to assess student results without controlling for teachers' use of the curriculum.

Staff decide to use a quasi-experimental design similar to the one used to assess the training workshops. Each time teachers begin a training workshop, half are selected as a comparison group. At this time, SHYSC staff give students in these teachers' classes an anonymous survey which assesses drug knowledge, decision-making skills, drug use in the past 30 days, and intention to use drugs (see Figure 5.4 for sample items). Two months after the teacher

Sheldon Heights Youth Survey*

INFORMATION AND INSTRUCTIONS

A research team at Sheldon Heights Youth Service Center (SHYSC) is trying to understand better some of the ideas, feelings, and experiences of young people concerning
drugs, alcohol, and certain other things. You are being asked to fill out this questionnaire to help them. This test will not count toward your grade in any way, AND YOU
DON'T HAVE TO FILL IT OUT IF YOU DON'T WANT TO. By doing so, you will
simply be helping the SHYSC people in their effort to understand young people, their
feelings, and experiences. Your help is much needed and appreciated.

Instructions: Here are some questions about alcohol and its use. To answer each question, please make a circle around the *one number* of the answer you think is best. Here is
an example:

Sample Questions: Which of the following statements about alcohol is true,
if any?

a. Alcohol is wet
b. Alcohol is usually eaten between slices of bread
c. Alcohol makes a person's hair turn green.
d. All the above statements are true.
e. Only a and c are true.

Now go ahead with the test.

1. A person can sober up by doing which of the following?

a. Letting time pass.
b. Drinking lots of black coffee.
c. Taking a cold shower.
d. Running around the block.
e. All of these.

2. Although alcohol has little nutritional value, it does contain many:

a. Proteins.
b. Calories.
c. Minerals.
d. Vitamins.
e. None of these.

*Adapted from "Here's Looking at You! A Survey of the Ideas and Experiences of
Youth" (Educational Service District 121, Seattle, Washington, and Washington State
University, Pullman, Washington), and "Drug and Alcohol Survey," Eric Schaps, The
Napa Project (Pacific Institute for Research and Evaluation, Napa, California).

FIGURE 5.4   Sample Items from Drug Knowledge Survey

3. During the *PAST THIRTY DAYS,* how many times did you:

	Not at all	1-2 times	1-2 times a week	3-4 times a week	Nearly every day
a. Use heroine or morphine (smack, junk).	1	2	3	4	5
b. Take barbiturates or tran- quilizers (sleeping pills, downers, barbs, tranks, soapers).	1	2	3	4	5
c. Drink alcohol (beer, wine, liquor).	1	2	3	4	5
d. Sniff inhalants (sniff glue, snappers, poppers, gas).	1	2	3	4	5
e. Use PCP (angel dust, krystal).	1	2	3	4	5
f. Take amphetamines or stimu- lants (pep pills, uppers, beans, speed, crank).	1	2	3	4	5
g. Sniff cocaine.	1	2	3	4	5
h. Drink coffee, tea or cola drinks (Pepsi, Coca-Cola).	1	2	3	4	5
i. Smoke tobacco (cigarettes, cigars).	1	2	3	4	5
j. Smoke marijuana (grass, pot, hash).	1	2	3	4	5
k. Take LSD or other psychedelics (acid)	1	2	3	4	5

4. Any situation might affect a lot of different people, but in the following situations please indicate your opinion of who you think has the *main responsibility.*

   Bill's father is an alcoholic. Bill isn't getting his school work done because of all the fighting at home between his parents when his father is drinking.

   A. Whose *problem* (main responsibility) is the unfinished school work? (Circle one)

      1. Bill's
      2. The father's
      3. The mother's
      4. Both parents'
      5. The teacher's

   B. Whose *problem* is the father's drinking (mainly)? (Circle one)

      1. Bill's
      2. The father's
      3. the mother's
      4. His boss's
      5. The community

FIGURE 5.4 (continued)

training workshops are completed, students in the other half of the classes are surveyed anonymously. This design is called a "separate-sample pretest and posttest design." Its advantages over a one-group pretest-posttest design are that students take the test only once, thus controlling for testing and regression effects (see Campbell and Stanley, 1963). Also, different groups of students will be tested throughout the year, thereby somewhat controlling for the effects of other events in the school that could lead to observed results. However, a difficulty with the design is the possibility that students engaged in drug use may be likely to drop out of school during the course of the year, thus favorably biasing posttest results. Staff decide to assess this problem by comparing the percentage of students in pretest and posttest classes who ultimately complete the questionnaire, using the roster of students enrolled at the time of the pretests.

The testing procedure yields 520 preworkshop (comparison) questionnaires and 500 posttest questionnaires. SHYSC staff have no way of handling this volume of information. However, they arrange with their evaluation consultant to use the data as part of a course she teaches in evaluation methods at a nearby university. Students in the course analyze the data using analysis of variance procedures. They find significant differences between experimental and comparison students on drug knowledge, decision-making items, and frequency of drug use during the last 30 days. SHYSC staff use these results to encourage other junior high schools in the district to participate in the teacher training program.

SUMMARY:
DESIGNS FOR ASSESSING THE RESULTS
OF PREVENTION EFFORTS

In this chapter, we have seen two ways an agency can assess outcomes of its prevention services: (1) documenting client satisfaction and (2) documenting differences in knowledge, attitudes, and behaviors. A series of posttest questionnaires was used to document client satisfaction in the first illustration. In the second illustration, a quasi-experimental design was used in which pretests of drug knowledge, attitudes, and use were compared with posttest scores on the same items for a different sample of students two months after their teachers completed training.

The client satisfaction surveys provide subjective judgments about the program and how it has been useful to them, but few direct indicators of changes in attitudes or behaviors. The evaluation of the teacher training program allows comparison of differences in knowledge, attitudes, and drug use between students and teachers who have not yet received the intervention and those who have. While the design does not control for certain possible explanations for observed results (maturation and mortality), it rules out a number of other alternative explanations (history, testing effects, regression, selection), thereby allowing greater confidence that observed outcomes may be the result of the intervention than is possible in the prior illustrations.

It should be emphasized that none of these illustrations uses a design which allows the conclusion that only the program generated the desired results. Only a true experimental design allows for such a conclusion. Nonetheless, these designs were able to produce evaluation results useful for the purposes intended. None of the designs required that prevention services be withheld from anyone or altered to meet the needs of the evaluation. In each case, the evaluation was tailored to the program as planned; though, importantly, in both examples the evaluations were planned before the services were offered. Evaluation was integrated with the prevention program, not tacked on as an afterthought. Both these evaluations required that staff plan for the evaluation before the program. Without such planning, neither evaluation approach could have been used.

Prevention program evaluations can be somewhat more difficult than treatment program evaluations because the desired outcomes may not be observable for a long time after the program and because prevention programs may use indirect services and advocacy as intervention approaches. We have seen in the illustrations, however, that indirect and interim evaluations using client satisfaction surveys can provide useful information, though they do not allow determination of the ultimate effects of the service. We have also seen that indirect services, such as teacher training, can be evaluated by carrying out the evaluation in several stages. Clearly, longer follow-up periods would have been desirable in all of the illustrations presented; yet even without them, information useful for program planning and problem solving was produced.

REFERENCES

EMPEY, L. T. (1978) American Delinquency: Its Meaning and Construction. Homewood, IL: Dorsey.

HIRSCHI, T., M. J. HINDELANG, and J. WEIS (1979) "The status of self-report measures," in M. W. Klein and K. S. Teilman (eds.) Handbook of Criminal Justice Evaluation. Beverly Hills, CA: Sage.

SKOK, J. A. (1978) Evaluation of the Pennsylvania Youth Services System Project. Wilkes-Barre: Center for the Study of Delinquency, Pennsylvania Department of Education, Wilkes College.

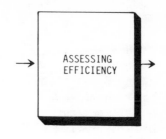

Chapter 6

ASSESSING PROGRAM EFFICIENCY

While we have just reviewed the process of implementing program evaluation in the context of prevention services, it should be apparent that effort and effectiveness were the primary goals of the evaluations. As you will recall from the description of the objectives-oriented evaluation model in Chapter 2, there is another evaluation goal which is related to assessing efficiency. Evaluating efficiency refers to such process activities and measures as work flow, volume, and productivity; work flow relates to client time and worker time, volume refers to the number of clients served and/or the number of services provided, and productivity involves ratios of costs to staff effort and time.

This chapter is devoted to a discussion of efficiency and the issues of financial costs in order to balance the heavy emphasis on effort and effectiveness found in most program evaluation activities. The fact that parenting workshops, teacher training classes, or counseling sessions are found to be effective may be insufficient information if efficiency is not also assessed. The past emphasis on program accountability from funding sources has resulted in a strong reliance on such efficiency measures as staff time and client volume. The future direction of accountability will most likely include a new emphasis on linking outcome or effectiveness measures *with* the process measures of productivity or cost ratios. For this reason, this chapter was designed to familiarize staff and board members with the process of costing services as part of an overall program evaluation. While the program may be viewed as effective with a particular client population, how much did it cost per client or per unit of service? Computing and analyzing costs are activities which staff and board members need to understand and complete with the assistance of agency management.

Sometimes very simple statements are made about agency program costs. For example, "It costs $52.00 per day for a client to be in our residential drug treatment program," or "It costs $150 to make a drug abuse presentation at the local PTA." What do these costs really mean? In the case of the residential drug abuse treatment program, the statement could have at least three different meanings: (1) that if one more client were added to the program, it would cost the agency an additional $52 per day, or (2) that the agency would save $52 per day if one client fewer were in the program, or (3) that the total costs of the agency for the whole year averaged out to $52 per client per day. In the case of the drug abuse presentation, the statement could refer to the cost of one additional presentation, or to the average cost of developing and delivering a series of presentations. What should these statements mean, and what role can this information play in an evaluation study?

When evaluating overall performance, the concept of average cost might be relevant, in which the total costs of the program for a period is divided by the total number of service units (client days or drug abuse presentations for the year). On the other hand, when deciding on providing additional services or reducing the level of services, other types of cost statistics are required. In the following sections we have defined some different types of costs that are useful in evaluating program efficiency.

DIRECT AND INDIRECT COSTS

Direct costs usually refer to the costs of an agency that are directly related to a particular program or service. The salaries paid to caseworkers, the costs of telephones, and other materials or services used in the caseworkers' program are all examples of direct costs. Indirect costs, on the other hand, cannot be directly attributed to any one program or service but are part of the total costs of the agency. The cost of the receptionist, the administrator, the accounting department, and fund-raising are examples of indirect costs.

The distinction between direct and indirect costs is very important to both funding sources and agency management interested in how much the agency is spending directly on services, and how much is being spent for indirect or supporting purposes. Funding organizations may perceive a low ratio of direct/indirect costs as indicating that too much of their money is being used for non-program-related purposes when looking at the same type of service provided in different agencies.

There is no single ideal direct/indirect cost ratio for human service agencies. Further, if the ratio is different from one organization to the next, it does not mean that good services are being provided in one and not the other, nor does it mean that the management of the one organization is more wasteful and inefficient. But by examining the ratio and the actual costs comprising the ratio, staff and board members can begin to draw conclusions about agency performance, thus contributing to the overall evaluations of the agency. Note that consistency, both between agencies and from period to perior within the same agency, is important in this analysis. Standardization of cost reporting is encouraged by the United Way and other organizations through issuing guidelines for agencies to follow.

VARIABLE AND FIXED COSTS

Variable and fixed costs refer to the volume of services being provided. If a category of cost goes up or down with the level of service volume, the cost is called *variable*. If a category of cost remains constant regardless of the level of services being provided, it would be considered a *fixed cost*. In human service agencies few costs can be considered purely variable or fixed. For example, the cost of meals and laundry in the residential drug abuse treatment program would be examples of variable costs, where the total cost to the agency for these items will vary directly with the number of persons in the program. The salary of the program director, on the other hand, would be a fixed cost because it does not vary directly with the number of persons in the program.

Most agencies must operate with a high proportion of fixed costs. Administrative and staff salaries, occupancy costs, and supplies and materials are all basically fixed costs, in that they do not vary directly with the level of services. As the demand for services increases, it is not likely that additional staff will be hired unless the increased demand is seen as rather permanent and increased funding is available. Likewise, when the demand for services goes down, it is not likely that staff will be dismissed unless the reduction in demand is seen as rather permanent and/or funding is not available.

The distinction between fixed and variable costs is crucial to answering questions such as, "If the program is effective, what would it cost to add one more client to the residential care program?" The answer may be very important when trying to obtain additional funding for the program or in setting rates for services. The additional funds sought or rates to be set should at least cover the additional (variable) costs of adding services, so that present services are not adversely affected.

For example, suppose that in the case of the residential drug treatment program, a request were made to expand services for ten additional clients. Is the rate of $52 per client per day still accurate? The key to the analysis is to compare the total costs of the present program with the total anticipated costs.

	Program at Present		Program Planned		Differential	
	Total Cost	Cost per Client Day*	Total Cost	Cost per Client Day*	Total Cost	Cost per Client Day*
Total	$475,000	$52	$551,000	$43	$ 76,000	$21
Total	$475,000	*$52*	$551,000	*$43*	$ 76,000	*$21*
Variable cost	142,000	15	209,000	16	66,500	18
Fixed cost	332,500	37	342,000	27	9,500	3
Number of clients	25		35		10	

*Cost per client/day figured at number of clients x 365. All costs are projected for the next one year

FIGURE 6.1   Variable/Fixed Cost Analysis Example

The information in Figure 6.1 is based on cost data for the upcoming year. The total cost for expanding the program by ten clients is $76,000. The differential cost analysis shows that changes in unit cost (in this case, the cost per client per day) occur when the number of units changes. The *total* cost per client day will decrease from $52/day to $43/day under the new program. Yet we see that taken separately, the *variable* costs per client day will increase slightly ($15-$16). The largest area of change in the cost component is in the *fixed* cost per client per day, which drops from $37 to $27 under the new plan. This highlights the fact that the expanded program will not result in any significant increases in *fixed* costs. This may mean that the beds, rooms, and furniture are already available to the agency. It also could reflect that no significant increase in permanent staff is proposed under the new plan. But the staff should be wary; perhaps the agency's fixed resources will be spread too thinly over the increased number of residents. A greater allocation of the proposed budget to fixed cost elements may be needed to maintain program effectiveness.

COST ANALYSIS RELATED TO EFFICIENCY EVALUATION

Cost information is needed in budgeting for programs and evaluating efficiency. If the agency has only one program and only one funding source, the problem is simplified, in that funds requested should cover the total costs of the agency at the expected level of service volume. If, on the other hand, the agency has many programs and many funding sources, the problem of analyzing costs becomes more difficult. Sometimes programs are partly supported by grants and partly by program fees paid by the users of the services. Such programs provide unique situations for the staff and administrator, who must ensure the quality of the program by analyzing costs and accounting for an array of financial sources. Simply stated, the problem is how to allocate indirect costs to individual programs, to ensure full coverage in budgeting and fee setting.

Two common methods for allocating indirect costs to programs in an agency are the *direct labor hour* (or work flow method) and the *percentage of direct cost* method (usually based on the volume of clients or services). The *direct labor hour* method allocates the total indirect costs of the agency to the various programs on the basis of the number of direct staff hours involved in each program. The *percentage of direct cost* method allocates the indirect costs on the basis of the ratio of direct program costs to the total direct costs of the agency. These methods are illustrated in Figure 6.2. Either method will serve reasonably well, but each does have its drawbacks, which should be understood.

The direct labor hour method may be inadequate for an agency whose labor hours are spread unevenly between programs. The programs with the least number of direct labor hours may not receive its full share of the indirect cost. The percentage of direct cost method, on the other hand, may result in some inequity if one program has unusually high expenses. For example, one program may require highly paid personnel in comparison with other programs. By the direct cost method, unreasonably high overhead costs would be allocated to this program because the employees are more highly paid but not necessarily to the amount of support services required for the program.

Using the cost figures for direct and allocated indirect costs presented in Figure 6.2, the administrator can prepare budget requests or set rates for units of service. When direct costs are combined with allocated indirect costs on a program-by-program basis, specific budget proposals or reimbursement rates can be analyzed to determine their impact on future operations. For example, assume the administrator has decided to allocate overhead on the basis of direct labor hours (Method A). Using the costs shown in Figure 6.2 for Program 2, we see that direct costs are expected to be $209,000 and indirect costs allocated are $30,906, for a total program cost of $239,906. If the support for Program 2 is less than $239,906, the funding of other agency programs will have to compensate so that the total expenses of the agency can be met. Often, if one program does not pull its weight, all programs may

Two Possible Methods

A. *Direct Labor Hour Method*

  — Total indirect cost to be allocated: $50,000
  — Direct labor (casework) hours by program
       (as forecast in agency's planning):

Program 1	1,050
Program 2	1,700
Total	2,750

  — Indirect cost per direct labor hour: $50,000/2,750 = $18.18 per hour
  — Indirect cost allocated to programs at $18.18 per direct labor hour:

Program 1	$19,094
Program 2	30,906
Total	$50,000

B. *Percentage of Direct Cost Method*

  — Total indirect cost to be allocated: $50,000
  — Total direct cost by program and relative percentages
       (as forecast in the agency's planning):

Program 1	$266,000	56%
Program 2	209,000	44%
Total	$475,000	100%

  — Indirect cost allocated to programs on basos of percentage if direct cost:

Program	%	Allocated Indirect Cost
1	56	$28,000
2	44	22,000
Total	100%	$50,000

Summary Comparison

Total Cost Under Both Methods

	Method A	Method B
Program 1	$285,094	$294,000
Program 2	239,906	231,000
Total	$525,000	$525,000

FIGURE 6.2   Allocating Indirect Costs

suffer. Note that under Method B in Figure 6.2 the total cost (direct and indirect) is $231,000. This is not to say that differing accounting methods can produce lower costs. The *total* cost to the agency remains the same under any internal accounting methods.

One of the biggest problems in allocating indirect costs to individual programs is being able to distinguish in the accounting records between direct and indirect costs. Personnel costs are often the largest item of agency expense, and workers are often involved in both program and nonprogram-related activities during the day. Further, the relative amounts of time spent on program and nonprogram activities could change from time to time depending on census levels or service demand. This sometimes makes the distinction between direct and indirect personnel costs difficult to estimate.

Human service organizations have found the use of time sheets helpful for categorizing personnel costs on a regular basis. These forms, prepared on a regular basis, can be used to keep track of staff activities as they relate to client service, administrative duties, training, and so on and can help distinguish between direct and indirect labor costs. The direct labor hours and costs used in the analysis in Figure 6.2 can be derived from summaries of time-sheets which distinguish direct and indirect labor hours.

Figure 6.3 presents an example of a time sheet, with the basic elements necessary for developing related summaries and reports. This time sheet, prepared twice a month, is flexible enough to allow for coding of different types of services rendered or different programs in which the staff member may be involved. This format may be of additional use as a data source for billing fees to clients or third-party reimbursement programs.

USING COST INFORMATION IN AN EVALUATION STUDY

This section includes some ideas for using cost and budgetary information as part of the overall program evaluation. For example, a program evaluation for a mental health agency might focus on evaluating the counseling program in order to plan for future programs, obtain data to present to funding sources, and develop standards against which future programs can be evaluated. Figure 6.4 represents a comparison of the budget for the entire counseling program, including its projected cost and actual costs. The costs of specific sample cases within the program could also be tabulated for a better understanding of the financial complexities of the program.

The following comments are an example of the type of budget analysis an agency might include in an overall evaluation report which includes information such as that contained in Figure 6.4. Our analysis of the actual versus budgeted cost information is presented herein as part of our evaluation of the counseling program. The actual cost was within $4,000, or 1.5 percent of the

Staff Member _____

Period _____ to _____

CLIENT	Day of Month 1/16	2/17	3/18	4/19	5/20	6/21	7/22	8/23	9/24	10/25	11/26	12/27	13/28	14/29	15/30	31	Total Hours	Service Code	Program Code	Client Code #
B. Harris	4			3														1	B	64160
K. Jones		8																2	C	40928
L. Meyer			2															1	C	20999
L. Meyer			5															2	C	20999

	Types of Service Codes	Program Codes
	1- Individual Counseling	A- Drug Crisis Intervention
	2- Group Counseling	B- Outreach
	3- Telephone	C- Vocational Rehab.
	4- Related Research	D- Other
	5- Other	E- Other
	6- Other	

Total direct program hours   4   8   7   3

Administrative activities   4   1   6

Other non-program-related

Holiday, vacation

Sickness

In-service training

Other

Total indirect program hours

TOTAL HOURS   8   8   8   9

FIGURE 6.3 Sample Staff Activities Form (Partially completed by staff member)

BUDGET[1]

DIRECT LABOR	Hours	Cost
Counseling		
Individuals	15,000	$135,000
Groups	4,200	37,800
Conferences		
With outsiders	1,900	17,100
With other staff	3,000	27,000
Training and Research	1,500	13,500
TOTAL (average: $9.00/hour)	25,600	$230,400

COMPUTING INDIRECT COSTS

Total budgeted for agency $= \dfrac{\$57,600}{51,200 \text{ hours}} = \$1.125$ per direct labor hour

Total budgeted for counseling program = 25,600 hours x $1.125 = $28,800

DIRECT COSTS	Hours	Actual $	Budgeted $	Over (Under) Budget $
Direct Labor Cost[2]				
Counseling				
Individuals	16,500	138,930	135,000	3,930
Groups	4,000	33,680	37,800	(4,120)
Conferences				
With outsiders	1,500	16,500	17,100	(600)
With other staff	3,150	29,650	27,000	2,650
Training and Research	1,600	13,000	13,500	(500)
Total direct labor	26,750	231,760	230,400	1,360
Other Direct Costs[3]		6,700	7,500	(800)
Total direct costs[4]		$238,460	$237,900	$ 560
INDIRECT COSTS[5]				
Indirect costs allocated to program		$ 32,100	$ 28,800	$3,300
TOTAL COSTS		$270,560	$266,700	$3,860
Total costs per direct labor hour		$10.11	$10.41	$(.30)

(continued)

FIGURE 6.4 Using Cost Information in Evaluating a Counseling Program (January 1, 1981 to December 31, 1981)

1. *BUDGET.* The budget is divided into direct labor costs (forecast by direct labor hours) and indirect costs (allocated by the total direct labor hour method). These budget figures provided the basis for the program funding from the United Way.
2. *DIRECT LABOR COSTS.* Direct labor includes the cost of salaries and fringe benefits for employees involved directly in the program. The breakdown of hours by counseling, conferences, and training and research categories was obtained from the staff time/activity sheets, which were prepared semimonthly by all staff. The totals also included time spent directly on the program by supervisors and other management personnel. Payroll records for the individuals directly involved in the program provided the cost information.
3. *OTHER DIRECT COSTS.* Other direct expenses included the cost of transportation, supplies, long-distance telephoning, and rent which could be directly identified with the program.
4. *TOTAL DIRECT COSTS.* (The sum of direct labor and other direct costs.) This amount represents a measure of the costs directly attributable to the program. However, if the program was not offered by the agency, many of these costs would still be incurred (e.g., rent).
5. *INDIRECT COSTS.* Indirect costs are allocated to programs on the basis of direct labor hours. Indirect costs include the cost of administrative and other support salaries, costs of general fund-raising, depreciation and utilities not included in direct costs, and other costs which could not be directly attributable to the counseling program. Total indirect costs for the agency for the period were $32,100, computed by multiplying total direct labor hours for all programs of 26,750 by the indirect costs per direct labor hour of $1.20. The budgeted indirect costs were computed by multiplying 25,600 hours by $1.125, which equals $28,800.

FIGURE 6.4 (continued)

---

total budgeted cost, which the agency considers reasonable under the circumstances experienced during the year. Indirect costs represented 11.9 percent of total program costs, compared with the 12.1 percent budgeted, which is also considered reasonable. The actual labor rates averaged approximately $8.66 per direct labor hour, as compared with $9.00 budgeted. This variance in direct labor cost per hour was due to (1) turnover of staff, resulting in lower than expected salaries on an hourly basis, and (2) some restraint exercised on salary increases due to unexpected increases in overhead costs.

The variation between actual direct labor hours and budgeted direct labor hours is primarily due to increased demand for service. This point should be discussed in the evaluation report but will not be included in this case example. A review of the comparison between actual and budgeted direct labor hours reveals that the staff apparently used direct counseling with individuals as the primary method of intervention, and that there were more conferences among staff than anticipated. In the training and research categories, the actual labor hours were high because of a greater than expected turnover in program staff. Other direct costs (mostly transportation costs) were somewhat lower than the budgeted amount due to fewer than expected conferences with those outside the agency.

Program administrators do not have complete control over the indirect costs of the whole agency. While the program exceeded its indirect budget by $3,000, the whole agency exceeded its predicted indirect costs by $5,000. This variance is reasonable in light of the increased demand for services realized during the year. Based on this review of cost information and other data obtained during the evaluation of the program, it can be estimated that the demand for services and cost of providing services will increase for the coming year. The number of direct labor hours could be expected to increase by approximately 5 percent to a total of 28,100 hours along with the cost per direct labor hour for the counseling program.

In order to summarize the major points on cost analysis and decision making, and to provide guidelines for designing or evaluating a cost information system, guidelines for a cost information system are presented below:

— Collect information on staff activities.

— Distinguish between costs incurred directly for the benefit of a client or client group and those that are indirect supporting costs.

— Collect costs relating to each case of unit of service, including a portion of indirect costs.

— Compute costs on a cost per client or cost per unit of service basis.

— Accumulate client costs by programs.

— Allocate indirect costs of the agency to programs according to a consistent method.

— Report direct program costs and indirect costs to program directors and administrators.

— Compare actual and planned costs as part of a report to the staff, board and funding sources.

These cost analysis guidelines are oriented to administrators, staff, and board members who desire a better understanding of agency funding processes. An increased awareness of the relationship between programs and related costs should lead to data-based decision making about the use of scarce resources in the delivery of services. The next section is concerned with developing systems and procedures for gathering cost and program data needed for conducting periodic program evaluations.

PROGRAM MANAGEMENT INFORMATION SYSTEMS

An agency's management information system (MIS) refers to the formal methods by which administrators and staff collect and transmit information needed for planning and controlling. The information produced by the MIS can include accounting information (i.e, per unit of service costs, current financial obligations), budget information (budgeted costs versus actual costs, projections, etc.), and service information (i.e., where do our clients come from, average number of counseling sessions, etc.). This information should be gathered efficiently and effectively through a systematic collection and transmittal process. An MIS can be tailored to any size organization, and for some organizations the use of a computer has been found to produce a wide range of benefits. Other organizations cannot justify the use of a computer, either because of cost or because the organization has no need for the vast capacity of most computer systems.

Often the impetus for developing a comprehensive MIS will evolve over a period of time through mounting frustrations on the part of administrators and staff in reporting information to funding sources. The MIS is a management tool for reporting how well the program is achieving its goals. If a program is expected to be cost-effective, the system would probably gather information on cost per unit of service for comparison with a projected cost, along with information about program effectiveness with regard to the population being served.

MIS information can be collected in several ways. For example, information on cost per unit of service might be collected by a combination of staff time/activity sheets using a chargeable hour concept, an expense-gathering system that would identify costs on a case-by-case or program basis, and a system for allocating the support services costs to each case or program. The "chargeable hour" concept is used for staff to report how they spend their on-duty time. Staff would show on a daily or weekly basis how much time was spent in what activity (e.g., direct service, administration, training, etc.) and the nature of the services provided.

Because the overall program evaluation process requires more than financial information, the MIS should be capable of ongoing program monitoring in areas such as changing client populations, changing staff activity patterns in response to short-term changes in demand for service, and the like. Figure 6.5 illustrates the possible links between the financial management and ongoing program evaluation uses of data within the MIS. On the program evaluation side of the figure, other sources of program evaluation information have been included to illustrate their relationship to the entire decision-making process of boards and staff.

The system in Figure 6.5 is built around several data collection forms common to human service agencies. With some adaptations, common forms can be used. The staff activities form (time sheet) noted earlier could be used for volunteer activities, client service patterns, as well as payroll, billing, and overhead costs. In this way, much of the information required for both financial and program evaluation tasks can be gathered efficiently at the same time, saving valuable resources.

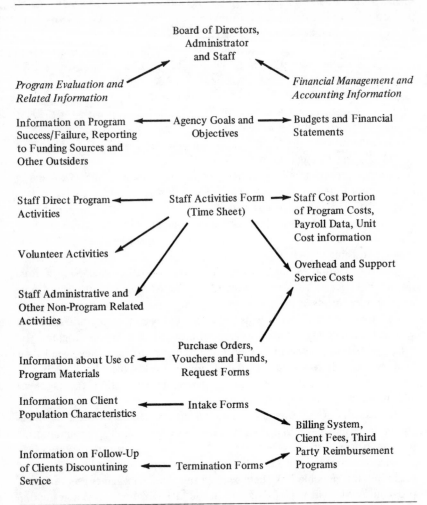

FIGURE 6.5   Illustration of the Links Between Financial Management and Program Evaluation

Much of the financial data related to budget preparation and monitoring can be efficiently produced by a comprehensive management information system. Such a system, which captures data on staff activities and program statistics, can provide information that is crucial to the controlling, planning, and budgetary processes. The use of an MIS can increase staff involvement in program evaluation through the use of improved internal communications on the progress being made to reach program goals and objectives. An MIS designed to collect appropriate information and updated to meet staff needs can contribute greatly to informed agency program decisions.

CONCLUSIONS

This chapter was designed to address some of the issues related to evaluating program efficiency. It assumes that board and staff members can use commonsense calculations to compute direct and indirect costs, understand variable and fixed costs based on information provided by agency administrators and accounting personnel, participate in decisions related to allocating direct and indirect costs, and keep track of work flow and volume of service data through the use of an information system. These issues have been linked by means of an overview of the relationship between program evaluation information and financial management information. While this chapter was also based on the assumption of no prior knowledge of accounting, it might be valuable for the staff and board to increase their understanding of agency financial management by requesting periodic review sessions with the agency's independent accountant in order to review and gain an increased understanding of such agency documents as the balance sheet, the statement of support, revenues, and changes in fund balances and the statement of functional expenses. Most United Way agencies have excellent literature for understanding these documents. While financial statements are prepared by accountants and administrators, they need not be mysterious documents for staff and board members.

REFERENCES

American Institute of Certified Public Accountants, Committee on Voluntary Health and Welfare Organizations (1974) Audits of Voluntary Health and Welfare Organizations. New York: American Institute of Certified Public Accountants.

ANTHONY, R. N. (1978) Financial Accounting in Non-Business Organizations: An Exploratory Study of Conceptual Issues. Stamford, CT: Robert N. Anthony, Financial Accounting Standards Board.

――― and R. E. HERZLINGER (1975) Management Control in Non-Profit Organizations. Homewood, IL: Richard D. Irwin.

GROSS, M. J., Jr. and W. WARSCHAUER, Jr. (1979) Financial and Accounting Guide for Nonprofit Organizations. New York: Ronald Press.

HALL, M. D. (1979) Cost-Efficiency, Cost-Effectiveness, and Benefit-Cost of Manpower on Community Mental Health Centers. National Education Center for Paraprofessionals in Mental Health.

HORNGREN, C. T. (1972) Cost Accounting: A Managerial Emphasis. Englewood Cliffs, NJ: Prentice-Hall.

MORRIS, J. A., Jr. and M. N. OZAWA (1978) "Benefit-cost analysis and the social service agency: a model for decision making." Admin. Social Work 2, 3.

SORENSEN, J. E. and H. D. GRONE (1977) "Cost-outcome and cost-effectiveness analysis: emerging evaluation techniques," in Evaluating Community Mental Health Services: Principles and Practices. Bethesda, MD: National Institute of Mental Health.

U.S. Department of Health, Education and Welfare (1977a) Evaluating Community Mental Health Services: Principles and Practices. Washington, DC: National Institute of Mental Health, Government Printing Office.

––– (1977b) Guidelines for a Minimum Statistical and Accounting System for a Community Mental Health Center. Washington, DC: National Institute of Mental Health, Series C, Government Printing Office.

––– (1976) The Design of Management Information Systems for Mental Health Organizations: A Primer. Washington, DC: National Institute of Mental Health, Series C, Government Printing Office.

––– (1974) Integrated Management Information Systems for Community Mental Health Centers. Washington, DC: National Institute of Mental Health, Government Printing Office.

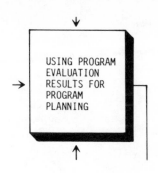

USING PROGRAM
EVALUATION
RESULTS FOR
PROGRAM
PLANNING

Chapter 7

PROGRAM EVALUATION AND PROGRAM PLANNING

By way of review, it is important to turn back to Figure 1.1 in Chapter 1 related to the reasons for using program evaluations. Our journey through the territory of program evaluation for the self-evaluating agency should be clearer in hindsight than it was when you began this trip with us. The following observations should have become clear by now:

1. Different "members of the agency" may ask different questions. For example, board members might be more interested in cost-effectiveness questions, while staff may be more interested in the impact of the program on clients. The reverse may also be true.

2. Program evaluation needs to be related to decision-making at all levels of the agency, otherwise evaluations become like useless computer printout—garbage in, garbage out.

3. Self-evaluating agencies require self-evaluating staff and board members.

4. Program evaluation questions should relate to one or more key measurement goals: effort, effectiveness, and/or efficiency.

5. Agencies need to assess their readiness for conducting program evaluations: timing, resources, interest, benefits, capabilities, risk-taking, and so on.

6. Getting started with program evaluation requires discussion and decision-making about one or more appropriate models.

    A. A Decision-Oriented Model

        1. What is the problem and who cares?

        2. Where can we get the necessary information?

        3. How good will the information be?

        4. Who will collect and report the information?

B.   An Objectives-Oriented Model
  1. Review of the agency's mission
  2. Documentation of program goals and description
  3. Specification of program activities and measures, as well as outcome activities and measures
  4. Specification of case objectives and case measures
  5. Organization of findings related to anticipated and unanticipated positive and negative results
  6. Interpretation of results in relationship to program planning and dissemination

7. Measuring the effort and effectiveness of services to groups as well as to individuals has some commonalities (e.g., monitoring and formulating questions) and some differences (e.g., different sources of interference and generalizability of findings).

8. Developing evaluation questions is an art and a science. The same holds for developing good evaluation instruments.

9. The sampling plan and study design need to be made explicit before venturing into the data collection process.

10. Data collection and analysis include several important procedures (e.g., informed consent, monitoring data quality, summarizing data, and statistical analysis).

11. The interpretation of data requires thought and risk-taking (e.g., carefully checking the completeness of the data, engaging others in the interpretation process, and being curious, rather than dejected, by negative findings).

12. Implementing the program evaluation process requires planning and the courage to get involved in an exploration process in frequently uncharted territory.

13. Program evaluation which emphasizes the measurement of effort and effectiveness is not complete until efficiency is also evaluated, especially program costs (e.g., indirect, direct, variable, fixed, etc.).

14. Program evaluation is an ongoing process requiring a mechanism and set of procedures to collect and organize data on a regular basis, frequently referred to as a management information system (MIS).

15. And last but not least, program evaluations need to be linked to the agency's ongoing program planning process, which is the subject of this final chapter.

These 15 observations provide an overview of the territory that has been covered in this guide. As noted in Chapter 1, program evaluations are valuable to a self-evaluating agency only if they are used. For some, use might mean modification in the structure or process of delivering services. For others, it may provide both anticipated confirmation of effectiveness and unanticipated findings requiring thought and consideration. While the discovery process has its own rewards, program evaluation needs to be related to ongoing agency program planning if it is to have any long-term impact.

PROGRAM PLANNING

The goal of program evaluation is not only to find out how one is doing or to justify what one has done but also to modify, change, or improve program effort, effectiveness, or efficiency. Sometimes it requires dropping what one has done before, creating an entirely new program, or considerably modifying and improving current programs. All these decisions and actions can be called program planning. Program planning takes place before we conduct evaluations, while we are doing evaluations, and after we have completed evaluations. But each of these phases of planning is somewhat different and each reveals different results. In this section, these differences will be described.

This overview of program planning includes a distinction between Phase 1 program planning and Phase 2 program planning, while acknowledging that in practice there is considerable overlap between them. The first phase of program planning consists of five steps: problem definition, policy formulation, analyzing and choosing among program strategies, program implementation, and monitoring/evaluation. Phase 2 program planning is divided into assessing the outcome of the evaluation and program development. Program development includes answering questions about who should be involved in planning and implementation, what are the "real" needs of clients, and how we proceed to set up a new program or make major changes in an existing one. The traditional separation between planning and evaluation (first you plan, later you evaluate) is not always realistic. Program evaluation is not, or should not be, separate from planning. The basic steps in the program planning process are shown in Figure 7.1.

PROGRAM PLANNING—PHASE 1

The first step in most planning processes includes problem identification and definition, preferably with the aid of some kind of "needs assessment" process (i.e., a problem not adequately defined is not likely to be solved). Needs assessment helps to determine the extent of identified social problems in a particular population or geographic area and is a useful tool in problem analysis; it is likely to reveal a discrepancy between problems as identified by professionals and those identified by clients.

In the second step, agency policy is formulated in relation to decisions about problems and needs: *Which* problems will be addressed, *what* will be changed, and *how much*? This part of the planning process is often carried out through the formulation of goals and objectives. Goals and objectives effectively become the policy which guides worker activities at the service delivery level.

The third step includes the examination of alternative program strategies in order to compare and choose among them. Both new and previously demonstrated strategies should be assessed in terms of their political, economic, and organizational feasibility.

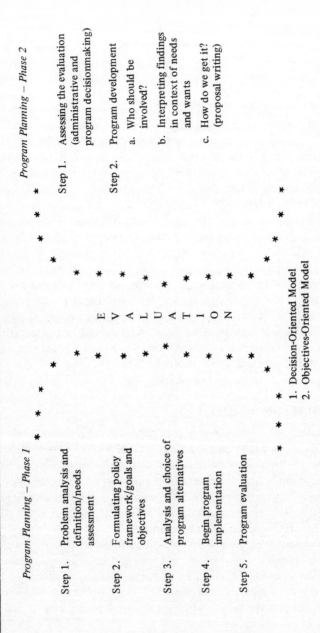

Program Planning – Phase 1

Step 1. Problem analysis and definition/needs assessment

Step 2. Formulating policy framework/goals and objectives

Step 3. Analysis and choice of program alternatives

Step 4. Begin program implementation

Step 5. Program evaluation

Program Planning – Phase 2

Step 1. Assessing the evaluation (administrative and program decisionmaking)

Step 2. Program development

a. Who should be involved?

b. Interpreting findings in context of needs and wants

c. How do we get it? (proposal writing)

E
V
A
L
U
A
T
I
O
N

1. Decision-Oriented Model
2. Objectives-Oriented Model

FIGURE 7.1   Relationship Between Program Planning and Evaluation

Some further planning tasks emerge out of Steps 2 and 3, such as creating specific definitions of services and service units, creating measurable service impact objectives, and establishing performance standards. A unit of service is simply an amount or portion of service that is easily measured and is intended to have a specific impact on clients. In a counseling program, a unit of service might be an hour of one-to-one counseling. In a "meals-on-wheels" program, it might be one meal delivered to one person. A service objective expresses how many units of service of an activity are expected to take place within a certain time, as well as the expected effect of this activity on the client. This specification process is the foundation for the objectives-oriented program evaluation model noted in Chapter 2.

In a sense, program planning—phase 1 ends after Step 3 because as soon as actual program implementation begins (Step 4), evaluation (Step 5) should begin as well, feeding back to staff information about how the program is doing in relation to the stated goals and objectives. This assures a connection between actual program operations and the phase 1 planning process. Services and budgets are continously monitored so that progress toward objectives can be measured. This feedback facilitates program decision making and inaugurates a new turn of the planning cycle.

Program planning, then, is a process which both precedes program evaluation and follows it. Planning begins before evaluation takes place and continues after it is over. As noted in Figure 7.1, program planning—phase 2 is the application of evaluation results in administrative and program decision making. What is the relevance of the evaluation results to the agency's programs? What decisions can be made based on the results? While we have moved from program planning, through evaluation, to program planning for change and development, in daily practice these separations are not nearly so neat.

An agency embarking on a self-evaluative course will want to examine *all* its current planning functions to ensure a proper "fit" between evaluation and the overall planning process. An important part of this examination is to determine the interests and needs of three levels of agency decision-making: policy, administrative, and service delivery. The policy level, often reflected by the agency board of directors, includes the review of the overall mission of the organization, including the organizational structure and financial foundation for service programs. Policy-level decision making involves long-range planning, the setting of priorities, resource allocation, and evaluating the achievement of agency goals and objectives. Administrative decision making, often reflected in agency directors and middle-management program supervisors, relates to the effective and efficient use of financial and staff resources to achieve agency program objectives. The service delivery level of decision making is often reflected in staff responsibilities and involves the day-to-day control and implementation of specified activities and tasks required to deliver services.

Evaluation is an attempt to enhance planning. It seeks to improve on the trial-and-error approach by assessing the impact of service programs *systematically*. Programs may fail to achieve their objectives because of failure in theory or in practice: Either a program was ill-conceived to begin with (i.e., it made some wrong assumptions), or it was well-conceived but not implemented as planned. Program evaluation aims to sort these things out and, it is hoped, reduce the number of failures needed to achieve success.

PROGRAM PLANNING—PHASE 2

In Figure 7.1 we also identified two steps in the phase 2 portion of program planning. The first, deciding on the relevance of the evaluation results, could also be conceived of as part of evaluation itself. Assessing the evaluation, Step 1, involves looking at the process critically to determine whether it produced the desired kind of information and in a useful form. It includes looking at the strengths and weaknesses of the methodology with the benefit of hindsight. Step 2 is program planning that involves actually putting the evaluation data to use by making a series of planning decisions.

One of the first program planning decisions is to determine who should be involved. If an evaluation has indicated the need for some major changes in an existing program, you will need to decide on what resources to draw. Whether to expand an existing service or to develop a new one is in itself a question of resources. Can these changes be made by a redistribution of effort among agency staff, or should other individuals or groups in the community be mobilized? In the case of a new program, should you develop it in collaboration with another agency? Are there other organizations in the community, such as the PTSA or another agency, which might be included in the planning process? Armed with information about program effectiveness, direct service staff can help develop linkages between professional and paraprofessional helpers and helping systems. The results of collaboration should yield a service delivery system that is more efficient, more effective, more comprehensive, and more sensitive to the needs of clients.

Once decisions have been made about who in the community should participate in planning a new program (or modifying an old one) and the evaluation findings have been interpreted for what they reveal about client need, then the agency is ready to go about making the program a reality. Writing a program proposal, whether for government or private funding, represents one approach to the phase 2 portion of program planning. The "program narrative" section of a proposal usually contains a description of a *plan of action,* as shown below:

1. *Statement of the problem.* What is the situation that concerns the planner and what makes it a problem situation? What is your evidence for this? Indicate who is directly and indirectly affected by the problem and where (geographically) they are located.

2. *Statement of objectives.* Contrast the problem situation with your desired state. What will be different as a result of the program? How will you know this and how long will it take?

3. *Spelling out alternatives.* Based on the literature or what you have learned from your own experience, discuss the intervention options. Justify your choice among them based on your conceptualization of the problem, the relative costs, and the capacity of your agency.

4. *Implementation.* Specify the program activities and the actual intervention techniques you will use. Also indicate how you will recruit and train staff and what, if any, follow-up you anticipate with clients. Include a time chart of *what will happen when* and a budget with justifications for each item.

5. *Administrative structure.* Delineate the lines of responsibility among your staff. If a community advisory board is to be involved, who are they and what power will they have? Provide brief job descriptions for all key staff, and if you know which individuals will be filling these positions, tell who they are and include resumes. Describe agency's experience with the problem, and staff competence.

6. *Evaluation.* Specify how you are going to monitor implementation and evaluate program outcome.

7. *Dissemination and continuation.* How will the results of this program experience be communicated to others? What are your plans for continuation of the service after this particular grant has run out?

In summary, program planning represents an important agency activity which precedes and follows the program evaluation process.

ASSESSING CLIENT NEEDS

One of the key issues that frequently emerges from both the program planning and the program evaluation processes is the dilemma of assessing client needs. For example, does our program fully meet the needs of clients? Do we have a good grasp of community needs in general and specific unmet client needs in particular? Needs assessment is a critical component of effective agency management, as noted in Figure 7.2, and serves as the focal point of this final section.

This entire guide is based on the assumption that the programs to be evaluated were developed in relation to recognized client needs. What happens when additional needs emerge and how are they documented? The truly self-evaluating agency must continuously monitor the presence of unmet needs which requires an understanding of the tools for assessing needs. Needs assessment is complicated by three facts (Warheit et al., 1977):

1. Human service agencies rarely have adequate resources to provide all of the relevant services needed in their communities.

2. It is difficult to know what services are most important, since community needs and problems are often diffuse and interrelated.

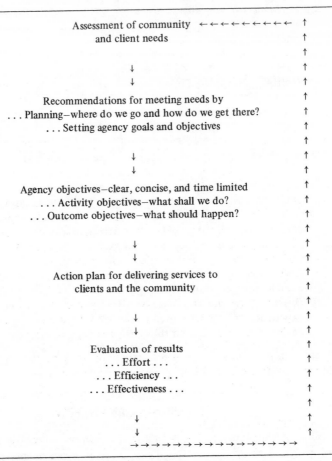

FIGURE 7.2   Agency Management Operations

3. The community served by an agency, and the agency itself, are constantly changing, influencing both the agency's capabilities to provide particular services and the kinds of services most appropriate for the community.

To overcome these difficulties, agencies need ways to plan services to ensure that they are likely to meet critical client needs. Information is needed on the nature and severity of existing community problems, the availability of existing community resources, and on what services have been effective elsewhere. In an effort to collect and use information to inform program planning, we will describe three categories of needs assessment relevant to program planning and grounded on different assumptions about goals: (1) program planning to meet perceived community needs, (2) program planning to increase agency legitimacy and visibility, and (3) program planning to prevent identified problems.

In program planning it is important to decide whether or not meeting perceived community needs, agency visibility, or preventing the problem has priority. Different techniques for collecting information in the planning process are likely to lead to service programs which achieve different goals. Information collection approaches such as community needs assessment surveys are excellent sources of information if the goal is to develop services that meet the perceived needs of community members. However, the information provided by such surveys may be of little use for developing services to prevent a specific problem in the community, such as delinquency. Once the general goal of services is clarified, an appropriate information-gathering strategy can be selected as a base for planning services that will achieve that goal. Approaches to collecting information for program planning are reviewed below according to the general planning goal for which they are of most use.

PROGRAM PLANNING TO MEET PERCEIVED COMMUNITY NEEDS

If the major goal of services is to meet the perceived needs of a community, then two information collection approaches are most appropriate: the community forum and the community survey. In contrast to other information collection procedures, both of these approaches go directly to community people for information. They do not rely on the judgments of "experts" or service providers whose responses are likely to be filtered through professional perspectives.

The community forum

The community forum uses a series of public meetings open to residents of a target area to gather information on perceived needs and services in the community. Forums may also be held for a particular target population, such as parents of primary school students or single parents of preschool children, whose needs are of concern to an agency.

The steps in this information collection approach are shown below (Warheit et al., 1977):

1. Clarify and operationalize the objectives of the meeting(s).
2. Identify questions to be addressed in the meeting(s) which will elicit spontaneous and candid responses regarding needs and issues.
3. Select a location for the meeting(s) convenient to the target population.
4. Publicize the meeting(s) in ways most likely to catch the attention of the desired target population.
5. Structure the meeting(s) to ensure participation (for example, following large group introductions where issues and objectives are identified, provide for small group sessions where more people will be able to contribute actively).

6. Structure information-gathering and recording procedures (designate people to record information exchanged during the sessions and, if desired, ask participants to respond to prepared checklists of needs/service priorities).
7. Summarize information, noting issues on which consensus was achieved and special emphasis was placed.
8. Develop action plans based on results.

Following the preceding steps will provide information that can be used to plan services to meet perceived community needs. There are advantages (e.g., inexpensive, easily planned and implemented, and allows for active citizen input) and disadvantages (e.g., articulate citizens may not be representative of community, may deteriorate into grievance sessions, may raise expectations about the agency's service delivery capacity, and the difficulty of determining the representativeness of the information collected) to the community forum approach.

While the disadvantages cited above can be minimized by planning, widespread publicity, and good organization and control of the meetings, the community forum *does not provide a truly representative sample* of community opinions regarding needs and service priorities.

One aspect of the community forum makes it potentially useful as a planning tool where the overall goals include agency visibility and legitimacy. By providing participatory roles for citizen activists, this approach may stimulate community support for program services that are designed to meet the needs identified through the forum.

The community survey

When carefully planned and implemented, the community survey can provide more valid and reliable information about community needs than the community forum. In the survey, information is collected from a representative sample of the specified population. This approach overcomes the problem of nonrepresentation of the population noted as a disadvantage in the community forum approach.

A community survey need not be large, complex, or expensive, especially if a limited target population (e.g., single parents of preschool children) is identified. The basic steps of community surveys are similar to the planning and implementation of program evaluation questionnaires noted in Appendix B.

An important consideration in planning community surveys is the possible involvement of other agencies in the project. Unless the target population is narrowly defined, it is likely that other agencies will also serve them. The cost of needs survey can be shared through interagency collaboration. Costs, time requirements, resources, and potential low response rate are disadvantages that should be considered from the start. The advantages gained from collecting valid and reliable information must be balanced with realistic considerations of what the agency can accomplish without compromising its ongoing services.

If properly planned and implemented, the community survey is the best information-gathering technique for identifying perceived needs of community members. It provides an excellent basis for planning new services.

PROGRAM PLANNING TO INCREASE
AGENCY LEGITIMACY AND VISIBILITY

While not often publicly acknowledged, agency survival may be a major goal of programs designed to give the agency visibility and legitimacy in order to ensure community support and funding. We have noted that the community forum and community surveys can be accompanied by publicity campaigns which lead to greater agency visibility. However, where the major goal is agency survival, two information-gathering approaches are even more useful in planning: (1) the key informant feasibility study and (2) the rates of participation assessment.

The key informant feasibility study

This approach seeks to involve a limited number of community members thought to be important either because of their special knowledge, status, or power or their resources. These key informants are asked to help the agency identify the most pressing needs of the community and to assess the feasibility of several strategies for addressing these needs. Key informants may be elected officials or organizational leaders, service providers such as doctors or therapists, agency administrators, citizen board members who have an "active interest" in a particular problem area, and clients or potential clients who may represent community groups. These are people likely to have important opinions about how services are currently being utilized and what needs are not being met. Their opinions are important not only because they know "what is going on" but also because failure to attend to their interests may cause public embarrassment. Involving them can generate important financial, political, or programmatic support for a new program. The key informant feasibility study can quickly identify problems that are likely to become public issues. It can identify the kinds of programs political and community leaders are likely to support. Finally, it can actively engage these leaders in the planning process, thereby committing their support to whatever plans emerge. It is therefore an excellent information-gathering approach for planning services that will ensure agency survival.

With the objectives for needs assessment clearly stated, it becomes easier to determine the kinds of people in the community who will be able to help. When both community support and meeting service needs are important, two sets of criteria must be used in selecting informants. A balance should be struck between informants chosen primarily for their power or influence and people with knowledge of community needs. A psychiatrist who specializes in working with adolescents, a clergyman active in his church's teen activities program, a law enforcement officer from the juvenile division, a businessman interest in a positive public image for his firm, a junior high school vice principal, an active PTSA member, the leader of a youth gang, or a city councilperson may all be valuable key informants representing important constituencies whose support can be important in inaugurating a new program.

Because the "sample" is usually small in using the key informant approach, an in-person or telephone interview is usually most desirable (e.g., high response rate, opportunity to probe, and maximum engagement of respondent with potential for subsequent involvement in program planning). In key informant interviewing, it is desirable to use an unstructured interview guide which lists topics to be covered and thereby can be useful to ensure comparability of results across interviews. General questions should be followed by more specific probes.

The meeting of key informants is an important final step in this process. In the meeting, data can be interpreted for program planning. The assembled key informants should be asked to spell out program planning implications of the assessment results. If consensus can be generated, the resulting program will have support from key members of the community. Thus it is important to examine and resolve inconsistencies in the results to the extent possible. If, for example, informants hold contradictory views about issues, these differences should be analyzed and decisions about priorities hammered out. The main task of the meeting should be clear: to translate the diverse opinions of key informants from the community into group consensus regarding promising initiatives for new program directions. The advantages are low cost and active citizen involvement; the disadvantage of the key informant approach is that the sample may be unrepresentative or out of touch with real community needs.

The rates of participation study

A second way to collect information that is especially useful for enhancing agency survival is the rates of participation approach. This approach uses information about people who have been served by the agency (or other service providers) as a basis for assessing community needs. Information already collected from monitoring and evaluating existing services is used. The assumption is that by analyzing existing programs' referral sources, client characteristics, services, and consumer satisfaction survey results, the service needs of the larger community or target population can be identified. Like other needs assessment approaches, the rates of participation approach has the advantage of low cost and use of available information and the disadvantage of missing the needs of people not already served by one or more agencies.

PROGRAM PLANNING TO
PREVENT IDENTIFIED PROBLEMS:
CAUSE-FOCUSED PLANNING

Perhaps the most widely stated goal of service programs is to help prevent identified problems. Some suggest that service programs can be effective only if they address the underlying cause or causes of a problem. To keep something from happening, it is necessary to remove or constrain contributing factors; for example, to prevent delinquency it is necessary to remove or reduce the environmental stimuli for delinquent acts or to increase the constraints, whether formal or informal, that inhibit young people from delinquent behavior (Cardarelli, 1975; Empey, 1978). This recognition leads to the third approach to program planning: cause-focused planning.

Cause-focused planning differs from need-focused planning in one major respect. It seeks to identify causes of a problem to be prevented rather than service needs in a community. Research has shown that perceived needs are not necessarily related to the causes of problems. As a result, addressing community needs identified in needs assessment surveys may do little to prevent the problem of concern. For example, a number of community-based delinquency prevention programs have used youth needs assessment surveys as a basis for planning services (see Skok, 1978). In some communities, these surveys have revealed needs for additional transportation and recreation services for youth. While these needs are real, programs which address them do little to achieve the goal of delinquency prevention (see Wright and Dixon, 1977). This is because these needs are not directly related to important causes of delinquency. To achieve the goal of delinquency prevention, cause-focused planning, rather than needs-focused planning, is necessary (Hawkins et al., 1979).

There are usually a number of wide-ranging perspectives about the causes of any problem. To continue the delinquency example, it has been argued that delinquency results when young people are not adequately integrated into the fabric of the larger social order. Others have said that delinquency results when people define and label young people's behaviors as if they are delinquent. Others have argued that delinquency results when young people are denied a sense of personal efficacy or power over their own lives.

Unfortunately, it is rarely the case that an agency can mount a sufficiently comprehensive program to address all the possible causes of a problem. As a result, it becomes necessary to decide which possible causes are most important in your community and to design a program to address them. Cause-focused planning seeks to design a program using the best available evidence about the importance of various possible causes of the problem.

While a number of the information-gathering techniques we have already reviewed can be adapted for cause-focused planning, there are two additional approaches: enlisting expert consultants and using available community resources.

Enlisting expert consultants

There are people whose professional responsibility is to study the history, origins, or etiology of various problems, whether physical or social. These experts usually work in academic or research settings. The assistance of such people can be enlisted in identifying the causes of the problem that have been shown by research to be most important, as well as possible approaches for addressing these causes.

It is unfortunate that people who plan and operate programs to prevent problems and people who study the problems often work in different worlds (Cardarelli, 1975). Universities and colleges should be viewed by agencies as resource pools to be tapped. Agency people can take the initiative to use the knowledge of academics and researchers in planning programs. The advantages of this approach include a relatively quick and inexpensive way to identify important causes of the problem and the potential for ongoing collaboration. The disadvantages include the realization that expertise about a national problem may not provide direct information about the immediate causes of the problem in your community.

Using community resources

A second approach to cause-focused planning is to involve local community members in identifying the primary *causes* of the problem in the community as they have experienced them. Lofquist (1979) has developed a guide for involving community members in prevention planning. Several of the methods for needs assessment already discussed, such as community surveys and key informant feasibility studies, may be adapted for this purpose. The important difference in the cause-focused approach is that respondents are asked to focus on *causes of the problem* as they see them, rather than on identifying *service needs* in the community. Their judgments are then used as a basis for planning a program.

The specific steps in this approach depend on the data collection technique adopted. However, in using this approach in cause-focused planning, remember that community people may not be accustomed to thinking about causes of the problems or sorting out which are most important. To assist them, it may be useful to use a tool to help organize responses. Figure 7.3 is an example of such a tool; it outlines 12 possible causes of delinquency and identifies prevention strategies appropriate to addressing each cause. The drawbacks to using community resources for cause-focused planning are somewhat similar to the problems that derive from using experts. Respondents may simply share their personal prejudices and perspectives in identifying causes. However, if they reflect on their actual experiences, they may provide valuable insight into causes of problems as they develop in your community.

By way of summary, we have reviewed three general ways information can be used in planning programs. Information can be used to identify commu-

1. BIOLOGICAL/PHYSIOLOGICAL strategies assume that delinquent behavior derives from underlying physiological, biological, or biopsychiatric conditions. They seek to remove, diminish, or control these conditions.

2. PSYCHOLOGICAL/MENTAL HEALTH strategies assume that delinquency originates in internal psychological states viewed as inherently maladaptive or pathological. They seek to directly alter such states and/or environmental conditions regarded as generating them.

3. SOCIAL NETWORK DEVELOPMENT strategies assume that delinquency results from weak attachments between youth and conforming members of society. They seek to increase interaction, attachments, and/or involvement between youth and nondeviant others (peers, parents, other adults), as well as the influence which nondeviant others have on potentially deviant youth.

4. CRIMINAL INFLUENCE REDUCTION strategies assume that delinquency stems from the influence of others who directly or indirectly encourage youth to commit delinquent acts. They seek to reduce the influence of norms toward delinquency and those who hold such norms.

5. POWER ENHANCEMENT strategies assume that delinquency stems from a lack of power or control over impinging environmental factors. They seek to increase the ability or power of youth to influence or control their environments either directly or indirectly (by increasing the power or influence of communities and institutions in which youth participate). (Efforts to increase community or institutional influence or power over youth are *not* power enhancement.)

6. ROLE DEVELOPMENT/ROLE ENHANCEMENT strategies assume that delinquency stems from a lack of opportunity to be involved in legitimate roles or activities which youth perceive as personally gratifying. They attempt to create such opportunities. To meet the conditions of role development, roles developed or provided must be perceived by youth as worthwhole (i.e., sufficiently valuable or important to justify expenditure of time and effort). Further, they must offer youth an opportunity to perceive themselves as either:

   a. Useful (i.e., youth perceives his/her activities contribute to a legitimate social unit the youth values).

   b. Successful (i.e., youth perceives he/she has achieved something desired, planned, or attempted).

   c. Competent (i.e., youth perceives that he/she has achieved mastery over a task).

7. ACTIVITIES/RECREATION strategies assume that delinquency results when youths' time is not filled by nondelinquent activites. They seek to provide nondelinquent activities as alternatives to delinquent activities. The condition which activities strategies seek to achieve (i.e., filling youth time with nondelinquent activities) is invariably met if the conditions of several other strategies (including role development) are met. Thus activities strategies are a lowest common denominator in a number of strategies.

(continued)

FIGURE 7.3   Typology of Causes of Delinquency and Associated Prevention Program Strategies

8. EDUCATION/SKILL DEVELOPMENT strategies assume that delinquency stems from a lack of knowledge or skills necessary to live in society without violating its laws. Education strategies provide youth with personal skills which prepare them to find patterns of behavior free from delinquent activities, or provide skills or assistance to others to enable them to help youth develop requisite skills.

9. ENVIRONMENTAL CONSISTENCY strategies assume that delinquency results from competing or conflicting demands and expectations placed on youth by organizations and institutions such as media, families, schools, communities, and peer groups which impinge on the lives of youth. Inconsistent expectations or norms place youth in situations where conformity to a given set of norms or expectations results in an infraction of another set of norms or expectations. This situation can result in confusion as to what actually represents conforming behavior and/or a cynical attitude toward legitimate expectations of any kind. These strategies seek to increase the consistency of the expectations from different institutions, organizations, and groups which affect youth.

10. ECONOMIC RESOURCE strategies assume that delinquency results when people do not have adequate economic resources. They seek to provide basic resources to preclude the need for delinquency.

11. DETERRENCE strategies assume that delinquency results because there is a low degree of risk or difficulty associated with committing delinquent acts. They seek to change the cost/benefit ratio of participation in crime. They seek to increase the cost and decrease the benefit of criminal acts through restricting opportunities and minimizing incentives to engage in crime.

12. ABANDONMENT OF LEGAL CONTROL/SOCIAL TOLERANCE strategies assume that delinquency results from social responses which treat youths' behaviors as delinquent. These responses may be viewed as contributing to delinquency almost by definition. The presence of social intolerance as expressed in the "black letter law," the actions of legal agents, or the attitudes of community members may be viewed as creating opportunities for youthful behavior to be defined as delinquent. In addition, such responses—whether in the general form of rules or in the more specific form of an instance of legal processing—may cause youths whose behaviors are so treated to perceive themselves as "outsiders," and consequently to engage in delinquent acts. These strategies seek to remove the label "delinquent" from certain behaviors. They take these behaviors as given and seek to alter social responses to them. Abandonment of legal control removes certain behaviors from the control of the juvenile justice system, thus preventing them from being labeled or treated as delinquent. Increasing social tolerance for certain behaviors decreases the degree to which these behaviors are perceived, labeled, and treated as delinquent.

FIGURE 7.3 (continued)

nity needs and plan services to address these needs. Information can be used to identify sources of community support for services and to plan programs to ensure community and financial support. Finally, information can be used to identify important causes of problems in the community and as a foundation for program planning. We have reviewed a number of specific strategies for

I. *Motives for Evaluation:*

Acknowledge the many possible alternative motives related to internal accountability and external accountability and decide which motives serve the immediate situation.

II. *General Advice:*

1. Expectations: Be realistic with moderate expectations
2. Bias: Control what you can and be alert to what you cannot
3. Scale: Seek to conduct small evaluations by dividing up potentially large evaluations
4. Abstractness: Direct program evaluations toward concrete, well-defined issues
5. Collaboration: Maintain moderate but continuous interaction between those conducting the evaluation and those who will use the findings
6. Risk: Reduce the risk of an incomplete or unused program evaluation by clearly delegating staff responsibility for completion and board responsibility utilization
7. Politics: Expect them and make the most sensible use of them (e.g., the politics of staff resistance or the politics of board indifference, the politics of funding agency accountability, etc.)
8. Success: Criteria for a successful program must be determined by agency staff prior to the program evaluation in order to have a foundation for assessing the findings
9. Timing: One or more program evaluations can be conducted each year depending on the size of the study (beginning with several small studies is better than one big one)

III. *Preparing for Program Evaluation:*

1. Identify specific, concrete program problems and issues (e.g., consider developing a brief, informal issue paper)
2. Engage in exploratory discussions and readings to get some feel for evaluation possibilities
3. Identify and interact regularly with the implementors and users of the program evaluation
4. Consider alternative types of evaluation:

   a. "Quick and dirty" approach using staff and board brainstorming techniques, available agency data, and intelligent observation and analysis for rapid feedback
   b. Exploratory problem-oriented approach using evaluation research and cost-effectiveness techniques described in this guide

FIGURE 7.4   Guidelines for Conducting Program Evaluations

IV. *Rules of Thumb:*

1. Make sure that the evaluation tools fit the problem and not the other way around
2. Carefully select and support the program evaluation team of staff and board members
3. Conceive of program evaluation as an interactional (or talking) and analytic (or thinking) process
4. Schedule interim reports to the staff and board on progress being made using intelligible language
5. Be sure to give equal attention to quantitative data (or numerical tabulations) and qualitative data (or case examples)
6. Utilize outside technical assistance only in areas where there is a clear need and only for minimal involvement, in order to maintain staff and board member momentum

FIGURE 7.4 (continued)

collecting information to achieve these three different goals. Using one or more of these strategies for collecting information can help to increase the likelihood that the programs implemented will, in fact, achieve their general goals.

CONCLUSION

It should be apparent throughout this guide that program evaluation can be characterized as an attempt to determine the value or worth of the use of financial and staff resources in meeting one or more service program objectives. Program evaluation as a process is not new. Informal evaluations using observation, fact-finding, and "guesstimating" continue to be the intuitive methods used by agency staff and board members to arrive at decisions. Our approach to program evaluation is more formal and less intuitive but still recognizes that the self-evaluation process is embedded in values, influenced by our expectations, and affected by the criteria we use to make judgments. We recognize that program evaluation methods are frequently unable to measure and verify specific "causal" relationships between the services provided and the outcomes reflected in client behaviors. We also recognize that the program evaluation process is somewhat like taking a picture of a moving target—the results are frequently blurred unless a high-powered camera or evaluation methodology is used. It should also be apparent that we regard program evaluation for self-evaluating agencies as primarily an art and craft and secondarily as an application of selected social science techniques.

While most of the program evaluation literature has been written for the program evaluator who is a specialist working inside or outside the agency, our self-evaluation approach is based on the premise that the best evaluations are not necessarily done by outsiders. While some argue that self-evaluation can be self-serving, biased, and impartial, our position is that all evaluations have some bias, are not value-free, and that outside judgments are not always more compelling then those made by persons inside the agency. Most important, we strongly believe that staff and board members responsible and accountable for program operations and performance should share the responsibility and challenge of agency self-evaluation.

As a conclusion to this chapter, we have modified a set of guidelines developed by Kimmel (1981) as a result of assessing the value and utility of program evaluation (see Figure 7.4). We hope that the guidelines and this guide have provided you with a philosophy and set of techniques that will be useful in conducting program evaluations within the context of a self-evaluating agency.

REFERENCES

ALKIN, M. C., R. DAILLAK, and P. WHITE (1978) Using Evaluations: Does Evaluation Make a Difference? Beverly Hills, CA: Sage.

CHASE, G. (1979) "Implementing a human services program: how hard will it be?" Public Policy 27, 4: 385-435.

DAVIS, H. (1973) Planning for Creative Change in Mental Health Services: A Manual on Research Utilization. DHEW Publication No. (HSM) 73-9147. Washington, DC: Government Printing Office.

KIMMEL, W. (1981) Putting Program Evaluation in Perspective for State and Local Government. Rockville, MD: Aspen Systems Corporation.

WARHEIT, G. J., R. A. BELL, and J. J. SCHWAB (1977) Needs Assessment Approaches: Concepts and Methods. Washington, DC: National Institute of Mental Health.

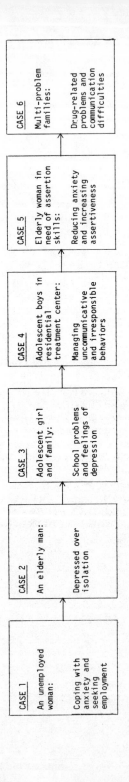

CASE 1

An unemployed woman:

Coping with anxiety and seeking employment

CASE 2

An elderly man:

Depressed over isolation

CASE 3

Adolescent girl and family:

School problems and feelings of depression

CASE 4

Adolescent boys in residential treatment center:

Managing uncommunicative and irresponsible behaviors

CASE 5

Elderly woman in need of assertion skills:

Reducing anxiety and increasing assertiveness

CASE 6

Multi-problem families:

Drug-related problems and communication difficulties

Appendix A

SINGLE-CASE EVALUATION METHODS

All direct service practitioners must make case-by-case decisions continually. If the information for making those decisions can be obtained in an organized and explicit manner, the value of the decisions themselves can be enhanced. This chapter describes a systematic data collection process for staff who offer direct services to clients. The case-by-case assessment of effort and effectiveness relates most directly to our model of objectives-oriented program evaluation. As you will recall, the objectives-oriented model involves the service provider with evaluating the tasks comprising the service objectives (see Chapter 3).

If you are a child care worker on the staff of a residential treatment center, a volunteer in an adolescent center or a day care program for the elderly, a professionally trained social worker in a mental health clinic or on a hospital ward, you constantly make decisions in your work with people. You use your best judgment each time, sometimes making comparison in your mind between this case and others, sometimes going by your intuitive sense at the time. In each instance, your decision about what you will do will be "tested" by the consequences (i.e., if what you have decided to do seems to bring about what you intended, you will continue with it and probably do it again with this client and with others; if it doesn't work, you will shift to another approach). We cannot emphasize too much the importance of the practitioner making case-by-case decisions and testing the evaluation process in order to obtain more systematic data for decision making.

SINGLE-CASE EVALUATION

Because single-case evaluation was first developed from a behavioral orientation, there is a tendency to view the procedure as applicable only to the behaviorally oriented practitioner. The case illustrations used here, and the discussions that follow them, are meant not only to illustrate specific evaluation methodologies but also to make one primary point: Whatever your theoretical or service orientation, as long as an objective of the work with the client can be articulated, then monitoring the outcome is feasible and useful. Particular client situations may be more or less amenable to outcome monitoring, but the methodology itself is not restricted to just one theoretical or service approach.

The evaluation methods suggested here are intended to put you, the practitioner, on firmer ground in the decisions you need to make by providing a way to check your hunches against systematically obtained data. Moreover, these evaluation methods call for specifying the objectives of your work clearly with the client and call for participation of the client, as far as possible and desirable, in keeping track of progress. Obtaining systematic data in cooperation with clients then becomes an inherent part of practice, and the client also has a better way of knowing about the progress of service.

The methods included can be done by an individual staff person alone or in collaboration with colleagues, and the suggestions specified will describe both kinds of activities. Illustrations will be presented to show how systematic data collection can fit into your ongoing work. Following each group of case presentations, some general discussion will attempt to anticipate and respond to questions raised by the cases. You will notice that the theme that runs through the cases is specificity—that is, clarifying the objectives of your work for yourself and, where feasible and desirable, for the client(s), the interventions you are using to meet these objectives, and the indicators that will be used to show when the objectives have been met.

The cases presented include activities assessing what is wrong in a situation, deciding what to do about it, receiving feedback directly from the client or through his or her behavior or expression of feelings, and having a sense of how the problem is being resolved. What is important in these cases is that indicators are now made more explicit, and the client is frequently included in keeping track of the resolution of the problem. The case examples will illustrate how this is done.

Admittedly, some situations do not lend themselves easily to evaluation, particularly with the client's involvement. The very young and the very senile client and psychotic patients are clear examples of such situations. In these or other instances where the situation calls for the client's active participation in or awareness of the interventions employed and their relationship to outcome, the practitioner may choose to consider evaluation primarily for his or her own awareness and as information to colleagues. The main point is that evaluation methodologies can be used selectively within caseloads, and for varied purposes and audiences.

The use of systematic data requires time and effort for the individual practitioner, at least at the outset. In the long run, however, these monitoring procedures may save time and increase both efficiency and effectiveness. For this reason, it is important that the agency administrative staff support the efforts of the individual practitioners both through general encouragement and through practical supports, such as reduced caseloads, as practitioners begin to implement monitoring procedures for individual cases. Peer support is also an invaluable resource in initiating these efforts. Practitioners can use each other on an informal basis for exchange of ideas and mutual support in dealing with problem situations.

In all work with individuals and families who are experiencing difficulties, the course of the case rarely runs smoothly and according to plan. This will also be true for single-case evaluation procedures. For illustrative purposes, the cases presented here show the methodology progressing in a fairly fortuitous way. This kind of presentation seems most useful in describing the groundwork of the methodology, but because real-life situations are often difficult, some problems in implementation are also discussed.

EXAMPLE 1: AN UNEMPLOYED WOMAN

You are a social worker in a family service agency, and your client is a 45-year-old single woman, Ms. Compton, who is experiencing great anxiety, particularly concerning her efforts to find employment. Your work with her is a combination of discussions to increase her insight into the factors leading to the anxiety and specific attention to job-seeking activities. The objectives of your treatment is to decrease her immobilizing anxiety and to encourage her to find work. Making these goals explicit with her, you decide to monitor two outcomes: lessened anxiety and job search behavior. You use self-report procedures for both, one focused on feelings and the other on behavior.

For the feelings of anxiety, you could use a simple scale, suggesting that Ms. Compton plot her level of anxiety on a graph regularly. A useful procedure for this kind of self-report is a "self-anchoring scale." You would set out a 5- or 7-point scale for her and explain that 1 would indicate low anxiety and 7 high anxiety. You then ask her to choose a phrase that describes her state at each end—for example, "I am so anxious and fearful I can hardly move," to "I feel calm and hopeful and ready to take on new challenges." She then has her own anchor points to decide at which point on the scale she would place herself at any particular time. You ask her to record her feelings of anxiety regularly, perhaps daily, and decide that you and she will use this information in keeping track of her general progress, and also in relating any changes in her disposition to specific circumstances in her daily life and to the content of your discussion. The monitoring could take this form.

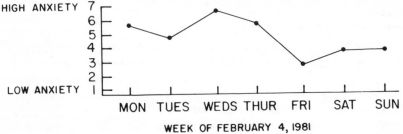

You and Ms. Compton could then consider the changes she reports within each individual week, and also over the weeks of your work together, and so monitor the outcome. If, however, the client's state of mind or your own intervention perspective precludes her active monitoring, then you might keep track of progress yourself on the basis of her behavior or statements in the interview.

The second goal, that of employment, might also be monitored by self-report. The client could note periodically the extent to which she has made efforts to find work. You might plan with her for a series of actions leading to employment (e.g., consulting employment advertisements, phoning or visiting employment agencies, contacting specific employers), and suggest that she note which of these she was able to do over the course of a week. The following graph illustrates her recordkeeping for a month.

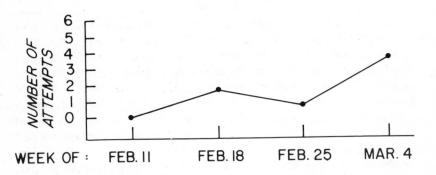

Both of these monitoring procedures, done by either the client or the practitioner, provide information about progress toward objectives. To address situations where the client's circumstances or your own interventive stance does not call for regular monitoring, a later discussion includes evaluation alternatives that have a different focus.

EXAMPLE 2: AN ELDERLY ISOLATED MAN

You are an outreach worker at a day care center for the elderly. Your client is a 72-year-old man, Mr. Fletcher, who lives alone. A public health nurse who visited him when he was recently ill reported that he is depressed about being isolated. He says he wants association with others but is fearful about venturing out. The task you set in your work with him is to encourage him to attend the senior center and to participate in some of the activities. With his agreement, you accompany him to the center the first time, but he says he wants to be able to get there on his own.

You enlist the help of the staff of the center in monitoring these outcomes. You set up reporting procedures for the staff similar to those used for Ms. Compton, based on their observations of Mr. Fletcher's attendance and participation. These data are useful in keeping track of his progress and in making decisions about the frequency of your visits and encouragement to him.

EXAMPLE 3: ADOLESCENT GIRL AND FAMILY

You are a social worker in a community center for services to adolescents and their families. Alice, age 14, and her parents have been referred because of school reports that Alice appears withdrawn and depressed and is doing poor academic work. In the initial discussion, the parents' main concern is Alice's change from a talkative, expressive girl to being sullen and quiet, in her room a lot, not seeing her friends, and not paying much attention to her school work. You sort out with the parents what aspects of these problems they can have some effect on, and you decide with them that Alice's uncommunicativeness is what bothers them most and what they might help to change. You suggest that in order to be clear about the extent of the problem *now* and to know *later* what changes may be occurring, the parents keep track of Alice's degree of communication with them over the next week. You set up a graph for them to use that will display the number of times each day Alice speaks with either of them.

The other problem the parents emphasize is the drop in Alice's school performance, specifically that she spends little time on homework and that her grades have gone down dramatically. You receive their permission to set up a monitoring plan with Alice's teacher and the school to keep track of completion of homework assignments, participation in classroom activities, and grade evaluations.

Over the next several weeks, the parents' graphing and the monitoring, arranged with the teacher, indicate almost no communication on Alice's part and very poor performance at school. The work with the parents now focuses on discussion of recent family stresses that might have contributed to the changes in Alice. You also use role-playing to encourage their attempts to draw Alice into some meaningful conversation.

You start to see Alice individually. She downplays the issue of communication with her parents, but says she is worried about her school work. She is just not interested in it any more, though she has been a good student up until now. She relates these changes to feeling alone, and that she feels her friends do not want to see her.

You decide with Alice that you will work on two issues with her: increasing the quality of her school work and decreasing the feelings of loneliness and sadness. For the first problem, Alice agrees that spending more time on homework assignments would probably help. You plan with her to keep track of the amount of time she spends each day on homework using a graph similar to the ones you have used with the parents. The two of you also work out a system for Alice to reward herself—with television time for example—for each period of time doing homework. Alice is aware that you are in contact with the school, and you explain that to know whether she is reaching her objective of improving her school work, you will also receive school reports. If their reports and her own do not indicate change in the right direction, you will need to figure out with her other approaches in your work together.

To work on the second problem, you work out a plan for the monitoring of her moods each day, specifically her sense of feeling alone and sad, using a simple scale and suggesting she plot this on a graph at the end of each day. Using a "self-anchoring scale," described above, she chooses phrases that describe her state at each end—for example, "I'm not good for anything, and no one cares at all about me," to "I'm really feeling high—everything's going well." She then uses these anchor points to help her in monitoring her feelings.

As the weeks go by, Alice's monitoring of her feelings and some actual steps she had taken indicate to both of you that there is a positive connection between the intervention you are using and a change in feelings and attitudes. This progress is indicated in Alice's monitoring.

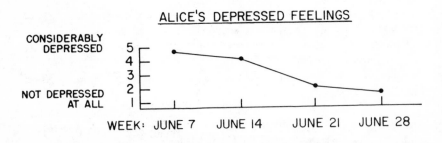

ALICE'S DEPRESSED FEELINGS

At this point, Alice is willing to be involved in joint interviews with her parents. Alice has now agreed with the family that increased communication is her objective too, and she also takes part in the monitoring of changes. In the beginning of these interviews, the emphasis is on the expression of feelings and the airing of some resentment. You and the family notice that there has been more improvement in the parents' charts at home, but that this has reached a plateau.

You then decide to institute some role-playing, rehearsing situations of family conversations, and this added intervention results in increased communications at home as evidenced in the monitoring. The next chart is an example from that period.

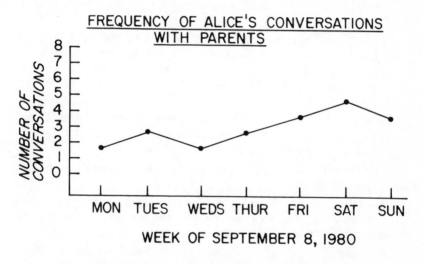

FREQUENCY OF ALICE'S CONVERSATIONS WITH PARENTS

WEEK OF SEPTEMBER 8, 1980

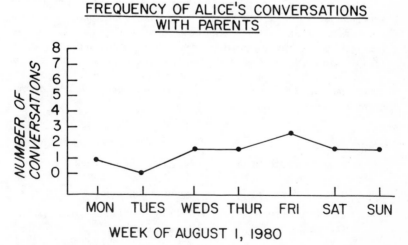

FREQUENCY OF ALICE'S CONVERSATIONS WITH PARENTS

WEEK OF AUGUST 1, 1980

There is general agreement at this point that the objectives have been met. There is better communication, Alice's school work has improved, she is feeling far less depressed, and the family has developed some skills for unblocking similar problems in the future.

Dialogue Concerning Examples 1, 2, and 3

The following dialogue between a social worker and evaluation consultant may touch on questions raised by the above cases.

SW: I had some trouble following these case descriptions because I would have handled these situations very differently. I don't practice that way at all.

EC: It's understood that there are many variations in the way people practice. These situations were just illustrative, but monitoring procedures can be applied whatever intervention is used. All that's required is setting objectives and figuring out some way to keep track of whether you're meeting those objectives.

SW: Well, for example, in Ms. Compton's and Alice's cases, I feel it's very important that individuals get some understanding of what has led to the current problem before we get to changing behaviors.

EC: Clear enough! What would you say were your objectives with them?

SW: As I mentioned, I believe it is most important that clients achieve insight into their difficulties and in this approach, taking measures every week seems very inappropriate to me. These understandings take time, and I'm more concerned about the final outcome.

EC: You might then decide to use one of the several measures of client-oriented outcomes. One possibility is goal attainment scaling (GAS), which focuses on the final outcome.[1] Goal attainment scaling can include outcome measurements for several goals in work with individual clients. Each goal is weighted differently for scoring purposes, depending on its relative importance in the case. This illustration will show the goal of greater understanding and communication, although in Alice's case the actual scale might also include school performance and feelings of depression.

	Scale 1
Scale Attainment Level	*Understanding and Communication*
a. most unfavorable treatment outcome thought likely.	Situation has worsened. Family has no understanding of each other and communication is less than before.
b. less than expected success with treatment	Pattern of communication has continued as before. Family has only a little more insight and understanding.
c. expected level of treatment success	Family has somewhat better understanding of their relationships and

	communicate at a somewhat higher level.
d. more than expected success with treatment	Parents and Alice show in interviews and reports of family communications that they have appreciatively better understanding of each other and are communicating more meaningfully.
e. best anticipated success with treatment	Family has great insight into their difficulties and relationships and are consistently open in their communication.

Goal attainment scaling requires that the practitioners, preferably in collaboration with the client, compare the client's situation at time of intake, usually including several outcomes, with a score at termination of follow-up. In Alice's case, you'd make an estimate of where the family was on this scale at the start of treatment, and compare that to a score at termination or at follow-up.

You could use the goal attainment scale at any intermediate point for corrective feedback, but in contrast with the previous illustrations, you would not be taking regular periodic measures. The emphasis remains, however, on specificity of outcome, concern with achievement of goals, and measures for the individual client.

There are still other choices you have for keeping track of outcomes, not necessarily tied to specific behaviors or feelings, and also not calling for a series of measurements as illustrated in these cases. These vary according to who provides the data and what aspects of the client situation are being rated. They can be used regardless of theoretical orientation and mode of practice. You may feel more comfortable with *these* if the illustrative measures in the cases appear too closely tied to specific behaviors or feelings.

Similar to the goal attainment scale is the global assessment scale. It requires the professional to make a rating of the client (from 1 to 100) depending on the client's place on a continuum of mental health. The lowest point indicates complete immobility and need of constant supervision; the highest, a symptom-free, well-functioning state. The rating is usually done at the beginning and end of treatment.

"Personal adjustment" scales are similar. They also involve professional judgments of client progress. These are usually done by an outside evaluator, ordinarily at some follow-up period. Though the time and expense may preclude these for routine monitoring, their main advantage is that assessment is done by persons outside the client situation.

Two other scales call for the client's input directly. "Client satisfaction" questionnaires are used to find out whether the service met client needs and to obtain the client's viewpoint about such issues as ready access to service, the responsiveness of staff, and personal changes achieved as a result of service. "Symptom checklists" also tap client evaluation directly. Clients rate themselves, usually at the beginning and end of service, according to how much they experience certain symptoms, levels of distress, and covert feelings. Sometimes direct service practitioners are not initially comfortable with the idea of using these scales. Let's return to our dialogue to see how this discomfort can be resolved.

SW: In any event, I feel awkward introducing the whole idea. It seems so mechanical, takes away from the kind of informal, sensitive atmosphere I like to create in my work.

EC: Yes, it's true it's a new and different addition to work with clients. I think you may find, though, that clients will interpret your attention to this kind of monitoring as an indication of real concern for them; that is, you care about whether your work makes a difference for them. You might tell them that research indicates that monitoring outcomes can help to bring about the changes people wish from service.

SW: The cases as you presented them rarely happen in real life. In your cases, everyone was cooperative and it all worked well. Most of my cases don't run smoothly. What do I do about monitoring in those?

EC: That's a very good point. The cases were written in order to show the process clearly, but I know most cases have unexpected turns. I'd like to speculate about a few possible changes in case situations that could affect monitoring and describe possible alternative procedures.

Now let's go back to the three cases we examined earlier. Each presents a specific problem.

Problem: In Alice's case, the parents and/or Alice either refuse to keep track of changes or do it so haphazardly that the data are almost meaningless. Also, Alice may refuse to come to the agency, or the parents may not continue if she does come.

Possible Resolutions: If some of the clients in a situation do not participate well in the monitoring, then you plan the monitoring with those who do. If some of the family members continue participating, but none of the clients is cooperative in the monitoring, then you might use data only from other involved sources: in this case, data from the school. There will be times when, even though monitoring is done, it is not done completely. Within limits, that's okay. For example, if Alice or her parents miss two or three days out of a week on their charting, just go with what you have, and of course, try to work out any difficulties that they are experiencing in the monitoring.

Problem: You have started your work with Ms. Compton, agreed to what you are working on and ways to keep track of changes, but the next time you see her, she is in a crisis because of financial worries and need for referral to community agencies.

Possible Resolution: You attend to the requirements of the case and make your professional decision about the client's needs in the crisis. If you work out a plan with Ms. Compton to spend time with her on the implications of the crisis, you might work out some objectives and monitoring techniques concerning the crisis. If the interruption is less serious and short-lived, you might treat it as just an interruption, and then return to the situation as originally planned, resuming monitoring on Ms. Compton's problems.

Problem: Because of severe emotional problems or retardation or other difficulties, clients just cannot or will not participate in monitoring. In fact, it is even hard to set clear objectives with them about your work with them.

Possible Resolution: Again, you do what you can. Clear, mutually agreed objectives and related measurements may not be in the cards here.

SW: It sounds as if there can be many variations in how this process goes along, but are you saying that, when it goes as planned, the monitoring procedures prove that what I did in my interventions brought about the change? From the little I know about social science research, cause and effect is a complicated issue.

EC: You're absolutely right. Even when social researchers are conducting fairly controlled research with large groups of subjects, they have to attend to many issues before they can feel confident about anything like a cause-and-effect tie between the intervention tested and the results obtained.

In working with a single case, there are some procedures that give one a little more confidence that the results came from your intervention and not from other sources. One method is to try an intervention, note the results, then withdraw the intervention (that is, interrupt your approach), and then start it again later. This is called a reversal design. If the desired results appear only when you use the intervention, you can be fairly sure the intervention made the difference. There are situations in which this procedure is both feasible and warranted—for example, in helping a parent to determine which of several approaches will really make the difference in changing a child's troublesome behavior. But in many instances, this technique may not be appropriate. A problem with reversal design is determining whether you can really turn off an intervention or whether in the reversal period (i.e., no planned treatment) the previous intervention continues to have an effect.

Another procedure for more rigorous testing of an intervention is to try the same kind of intervention in a series of different problem areas or in a series of different situations in which the same problem manifests itself. (These are called multiple-baseline procedures.) In Alice's case, you might use a particular intervention, like insight therapy or behavioral rehearsal, first, for her communication difficulties with her parents, then with the school staff, then with her personal friends. If the intervention works in each situation, then you can be fairly certain the intervention was what made the difference. All these procedures for determining whether the intervention made the difference should have baseline data for a period of time before you initiate treatment. The intervention must also be monitored carefully, to assure that in fact the treatment has been instituted as planned.

To increase confidence in your results it is helpful to establish the outcomes by using different sources of data. For example, if the parents, the school, and Alice herself all say that Alice's school work is improving, then you can be reasonably sure change has occurred. Also, if the parents keep track of Alice's work behavior, the school records examination results, and Alice reports on her feelings about the school situation, the combination of data enhances the certainty of the results. If, in addition to treating Alice, you handle other cases by using similar interventions and get similarly positive results, the results cannot easily be explained away by coincidence. Replication over a series of cases is an essential ingredient to having confidence in a cause-effect relationship. You can also use replication to find out at what point during treatment certain approaches were effective, and to determine whether seeing clients individually or as a family unit has an effect on outcome.

SW: Well, I see there may be some uses for all this, but it seems like a lot of work. I'm not sure about the time and effort involved.

EC: Of course, I'd have to agree about what clearly seems like extra work and complications. I'd like to emphasize that it's possible that some of the time spent now in frustrating discussions about the different decisions you need to make might be saved by a more systematic look at outcome. You might be able to make decisions more quickly, monitoring itself could hasten improvement, and you might switch interventions more readily when needed.

EXAMPLE 4: RESIDENTIAL TREATMENT CENTER CASES

Assume for the moment that you are a child care worker on the staff of a residential treatment center for adolescent boys. There are four boys with whom you are most directly involved, and you have different sets of concerns and different decisions to make about each of them. Many of the interactions you have with these boys each day are intuitive and unplanned, but in each boy's case, the focus is on a central problem, and there are certain actions you use in the expectation that these will have an impact on that problem.

Gene's main problem is serious depression. He is uncommunicative, does little school work, sits by himself most of the time, and his entire bearing reflects sadness. On the assumption that increased activity may counteract depression, you find out through Gene's family and the center's caseworker that he had been in the school band and you decide that you will spend time with him each day to see if trying to renew his active interest in playing the clarinet will affect his generally depressed state. You make two decisions about the monitoring. First, you will ask another staff member to make an evaluation of Gene's general emotional state as you try this intervention, so that your own involvement in the intervention will not bias the judgment. Second, though Gene is too depressed at the outset to take an active role in the monitoring, you will try to involve him as soon as his emotional state permits. The following graph represents the monitoring efforts in your work with Gene and illustrates Gene's later participation in the monitoring.

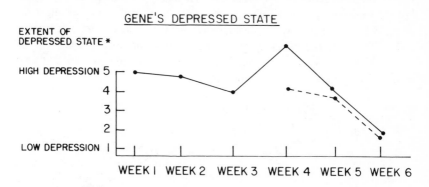

GENE'S DEPRESSED STATE

* SOLID LINE INDICATES THE EVALUATION BY OTHER STAFF MEMBER; DOTTED LINE INDICATES GENE'S SELF-REPORTS.

This same case might have a very different history. The activity-focused efforts may have had no effect on Gene's depression, and he may have been completely unwilling to participate in the monitoring. The measurements would have looked like this and you would have had to rethink your interventions.

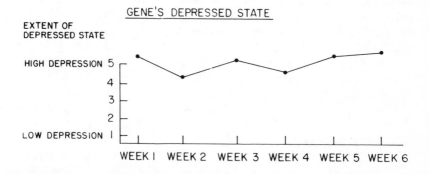

GENE'S DEPRESSED STATE

Negative results, though frustrating, can be as important as positive ones, because they are a clear indication of the need for a reconsideration of the interventions used.

Peter has had problems with misuse of his time away from the center. He has been given permission for walks outside the grounds but several times has overstayed his time and sometimes has been discovered shoplifting. The usual procedure has been to place restrictions on him when the privilege was abused, with the number and degree of restrictions dependent on the severity of Peter's behavior. You are concerned about the effectiveness of this procedure, particularly about how to use restrictions more effectively to change Peter's problem behavior. You set up a monitoring procedure that will reflect Peter's behavior on walks outside the grounds to see if any changes are affected by different ways of dealing with the behavior. The following graph reflects both Peter's behavior and your intervention over a period of six weeks. You have the graph available for Peter to see and he is aware of your efforts to help him control his behavior.

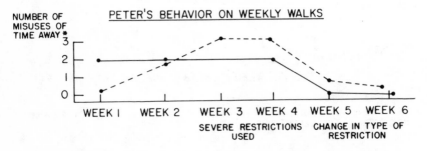

*DOTTED LINE INDICATES LATENESS (NUMBER OF HOURS LATE);
SOLID LINE INDICATES INSTANCES OF SHOPLIFTING.

During the first two weeks, you have continued with the restrictions used previously—TV time, movie privileges, and so on. Since the lateness and shoplifting continue, you decide to increase the severity of the restrictions during the next two weeks. You see that this has little effect on his behavior, and you are aware some changes need to be made in interventions. You and other staff members notice that Peter has developed an important relationship with a new resident and enjoys playing ping pong and tennis with him. You decide to use this relationship as a reward system for Peter, and tell him that the amount of time permitted for these desired activities is directly related to his behavior on time away from the center. If there is no problem with lateness or shoplifting, he can have more time with his new friend. Your monitoring indicates that this intervention during weeks 5 and 6 makes a difference in Peter's behavior.

Bob has a history of serious upsets on return from weekend home visits, and you are faced with the continual decision as to when and whether to allow those visits. Bob shares his ambivalence about the visits home and is aware that after each visit his school work deteriorates, he has difficulty in his interactions with the staff and other boys, and he experiences physical effects such as sleeplessness and loss of appetite. At the same time, he wants to visit and does not want to lose touch with his family.

You decide with Bob that you will try different ways to plan the frequency of visits and see which frequency works better for him. You will try visits every month for three months, and then every other week for two months, and see the effects. You arrange with the school to monitor his homework assignment performance throughout this period, for other staff to keep track of instances of problem interactions, and for Bob to monitor his own physical state. The following graph sets out the several evaluations of Bob's reactions to the home visits as the frequency of the visits is varied.

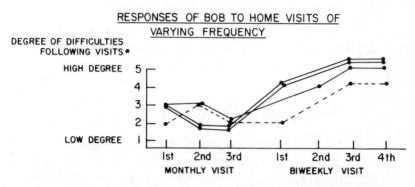

RESPONSES OF BOB TO HOME VISITS OF VARYING FREQUENCY

DOTTED LINE INDICATES STAFF ESTIMATE OF INTERPERSONAL DIFFICULTIES. SOLID LINE INDICATES SCHOOL'S EVALUATION OF HOMEWORK. DOUBLE SOLID LINE INDICATES BOB'S ESTIMATE OF PHYSICAL EFFECTS ON HIM.

With Bob's participation in seeing the results of the monitoring, you decide with him that monthly visits seem to have less serious consequences for him than those that are biweekly.

Jack has been at the center for over a year, and in the next few months a decision will be considered about termination. When Jack first came, he had few social or coping skills. He had difficulty in communicating with other people, could not manage himself at all in situations of conflict, could not meet school expectations, and was unable to make his own ideas and feelings known to others. You and other staff members have worked hard with him and are beginning to see some positive changes. There has been a staff decision that termination can be considered if Jack's skills continue to improve in at least some of these areas.

With the cooperation of other staff and school personnel, you decide to set up a reporting system on Jack's social skills development. The graph below illustrates change in two of the skill areas as monitored by two separate groups, the staff and school.

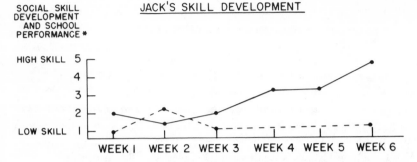

SOCIAL SKILL
DEVELOPMENT
AND SCHOOL
PERFORMANCE *

JACK'S SKILL DEVELOPMENT

* SOLID LINE INDICATES STAFF REPORTS OF SELF-INITIATIVE EXPRESSIONS.
DOTTED LINE INDICATES REPORTS OF SCHOOL PERFORMANCE.

Since the monitoring shows that there is a discrepancy between the staff and the school reports, you need to reconsider termination until the difficulties represented by the school performance are addressed. Because the school situation is more like the outside world than are Jack's interactions with staff, you decide he needs more help in transferring skills to outside situations and that termination should be delayed until some of that work is done.

In each of these cases, your work may be based on a different treatment orientation not so directly tied to specific behaviors. If this is so, you have other monitoring alternatives, as discussed earlier. You can use any of those more general assessments, tapping such areas as overall functioning and adjustment, in order to look at broad changes that occur over longer periods.

Dialogue Concerning Example 4

A child care social worker (SW) and a evaluation consultant (EC) have a discussion about these case situations.

SW: I know that at the beginning of these examples it was mentioned that child care workers do a lot of on-the-spot decision making, but I just want to emphasize that most of what I do is just that. All of these discussions make it seem that we are in a position to make more reasoned decisions than are possible. Besides, a lot of this involves setting down in a graph what we already know intuitively.

EC: Yes, I'm aware that this is so, and that these decisions and activities we've been describing are just part of your total job. Still, I believe you do have important and specific concerns about particular residents and that you try to make your behavior with them reflect those concerns. These systematic procedures are meant to help you clarify both the major problems of your clients and the success of your treatment methods.

SW: Many of these kinds of decisions you've been illustrating are ones I don't make on my own. The caseworker and staff members play a large part in the decision making. Also, other treatment is going on simultaneously with our work with these boys.

EC: Yes, I understand that's the case. Some of the monitoring procedures suggested here might be done jointly with other staff.

SW: When you mentioned having the boys monitor their own changes, several real aspects of our situation came to mind. Many of the boys here are so disturbed that we cannot expect them to take on rational, responsible tasks. Also, others have incredible abilities to manipulate people, and they could easily con us about progress. And then there are others who will do anything to please. What kind of real and honest self-reports can we expect from these boys?

EC: The kind of problems you raise are true, of course, among many clients and makes this process complicated and uneven. You can do a few things about the dilemma. Because you know the boys so well, you can probably make your own judgement about the reliability of the data you're getting from them. You'll know when to make every effort to get information from other sources to see if it coincides with what the boys report. In any case, involving the boys may bring about improvement, and gathering data from other sources will only make your evaluation more certain.

EXAMPLE 5: AN ASSERTION TRAINING GROUP

As a social worker in a day center for the elderly, you are offering a course in assertion skills to a group of older women. The purpose of the course is to enable the women to be more assertive in a range of situations—with their families, with their doctors, and with sales people, for example—without depreciating the other person and without feeling unduly anxious about doing so. You are interested in increasing their repertoire of interpersonal skills and decreasing their levels of anxiety. Though your intervention involves group processes (discussions about assertiveness and anxiety, rehearsals of real-life situations, and reports to the group about attempts at assertion between sessions), you are concerned that each individual will make progress in developing skills and understanding feelings.

At the start of the course, you use a standardized inventory for everyone in the class (e.g., Gambrill-Richey Assertion Inventory; Gambrill and Richey, 1975), which asks individuals to rate, across a number of real situations, the probability that they would act assertively and the degree of anxiety they would feel about doing so. After the six weeks of group sessions, you ask the participants to complete the inventory again. You then have the opportunity to see the self-reported changes in both acts and feeling levels, to know how each individual and how the group as a whole changed as a result of the group

experience. You can also share the two inventories with interested participants so they, too, can see the changes they have reported.

Dialogue Concerning Example 5

SW: I'm glad you have an example of groups since group work is frequently
part of my practice. I have two questions, however. One is that sometimes
the purpose of my groups is to bring about other kinds of changes, such
as increasing communication among family members or helping adolescents in their social interchanges with their peers.

EC: In those situations, you can either use another standard inventory for
those particular skills or develop your own set of questions using one of
the standard forms as a guide.

SW: My other question is about the kind of groups I often conduct in which
each individual is working on his or her own particular problem, so that
there are no standardized goals. Also, the goals are frequently psychological in nature—for example, feeling more sure or less depressed, or gaining
insight.

EC: To keep track of individual progress on varied goals, you might use the
goal attainment scaling mentioned earlier and fashion individual indicators for each person's progress. You could see simple self-report forms to
monitor these. And if the goals were psychological ones primarily, you
would focus on these kinds of changes in your inquiry and in your
goal-setting.

If your group occurs in an institutional setting, you could ask for
corroborating data from other professionals or paraprofessionals there,
such as nurses or doctors, child care workers, hospital aides, or occupa-
tional therapists.

SW: Sometimes I'm concerned also with the progress of the group as a whole,
what changes occur in the group dynamics.

EC: You might then seek feedback from the group about just that. For
example, you could use sociometric measures that get at changes of
status of group members, or get reports from the group members on a
simple questionnaire about their view of changes in interrelationships in
the group or about interpersonal changes.

Other Measures

The following example illustrates the use of data collection, not for
outcome measurement but for planning better services. This example makes
two points: (1) Staff can initiate the use of systematic data collection to
have an impact on agency function; and (2) in addition to the evaluation of
individual cases, staff can be involved with their colleagues in a joint venture
of utilizing data to meet a specific purpose.

EXAMPLE 6: PRACTITIONER-INITIATED GROUP EVALUATION

As a member of a large staff in a community agency serving adolescents and their families, you notice that certain adolescents with one or both of their parents repeatedly drop in to present the same problem but never follow through on a continuing basis. You think that instead of individual services, specific groups focusing on particular problems might be a more effective intervention. You have a hunch a few types of problems show up more often than others, but you are not sure.

You find that others on the staff would also like to suggest to the agency administration that they plan for a few special focus groups, but since there has been a previous history of little client enthusiasm for planned groups, you want data to back up your argument before you present your suggestion.

You and your colleagues decide you will keep track of individuals who drop in over the next four months to see if there is a relationship between the type of problems and the frequency of the sporadic return visits. From your combined experience, your group develops a list of frequent problem situations and spends time agreeing on definitions of items on the list. Each person has a copy of the list and agrees to keep track of the times a family with a particular problem drops in over the next four months. You agree to pool the information at the end of that time. The pooled data looks like this.

TABLE A.1 Patterns of Problems and Frequency of Drop-In Visits

			Types of Problems		
Frequency of Visits	*Drug-Related*	*School Problems*	*Family Communication*	*Runaways*	*Adolescents Depression*
	No. (%)	No. (%)	No. (%)	No. (%)	No. (%)
One visit	12 (19)	22 (55)	8 (14)	10 (28)	17 (38)
Two visits	15 (24)	8 (20)	12 (21)	14 (40)	10 (22)
Three or more visits	35 (57)	10 (25)	38 (65)	11 (32)	18 (40)
Total	62 (100)	40 (100)	58 (100)	35 (100)	45 (100)

The data indicate that families with drug-related problems (57 percent of these) and communication difficulties (65 percent of these) have had the most sporadic visits. You and your colleagues believe there is a good case to be made for planning two groups to be offered by the agency and you believe you are ready, fortified with your data, to make a presentation at the next staff meeting.

Dialogue Concerning Example 6

SW: As you were describing this, my first thought was that the agency administration should be spending the time and effort to do this kind of data gathering. This is an agency responsibility and the staff should not have to use their energies for this.

EC: I agree that this has to do with overall agency planning, and in some situations the problem can be raised by the staff and the agency might agree it was an important issue and proceed with the survey. I can see several advantages, though, in staff being ready to take on the task. First, an agency might not have the resources and the survey will be put off. If you can organize even a small effort, you and your colleagues don't have to wait. Second, the methods of the data collection reflect your needs and your experience in direct work with clients. Third, by carrying through such a project, your efforts, reflecting your perspective, can have an immediate impact on agency directions.

SW: That's a good point. Evaluating and effecting new treatments gets a lot more done than griping about the agency. In a practical sense, though, it seems we might have difficulty agreeing on what problems to include and deciding which family goes in which category. Sometimes there's more than one problem reported for each client.

EC: You need consensus on the major problems to include, but if there are some staff who think you may be excluding some important problems, just set up an "other" category. You can see later whether that category catches a problem that should be included. For the multiple problem situations, you may just need to agree to have each person use his or her own judgment as to which problem seemed the most pressing and use that category. Researchers often find that problem definition is the most interesting, and you and your colleagues may find you learn a lot about each other's ideas and practice as you go through this phase of your study.

SW: Some of us who started this project might be more committed to it and be more consistent in our monitoring, and others might not be. We might not be getting uniform data from the several people involved.

EC: That might be a problem even if you were doing a rigorous research design. For your purposes, the chances are good that the information will generally reflect the state of affairs and, most important, will be considerably more effective than your individual hunches.

The major point of this appendix may very well be reflected in the evaluation consultant's last comment. Practitioners are continually making decisions based on accumulated wisdom, intuition, and hunches. These can be valuable sources, but the practitioner's use of systematic data for decision making (with data collection originating in their own offices or the offices of their colleagues) allows them a role in increasing the effectiveness of service.

NOTE

1. Goal attainment scaling is just one of a number of client-oriented outcome indices. For a discussion of several of these, see NIMH Manual (Little). (For fuller discussions of goal attainment scaling, see Kiresuk, 1973, 1975; Seaberg and Gillespie, 1977.)

REFERENCES

BRIAR, S. (1973) "Effective social work intervention in direct practice: implications for education," In Facing the Challenge, Council for Social Work Education.

GAMBRILL, E. D. and C. A. RICHEY (1975) Behavior Therapy.

GUTTMAN, J. and S. LEIBLUM (1974) How to do Psychotherapy and How to Evaluate It. New York: Holt, Rinehart & Winston. (See especially Chapters 4, 5, 15.)

HOWE, M. W. (1974) "Casework self-evaluation: a single-subject approach." Social Service Review March: 1-23.

MUTSCHLER, E. (1979) "Using single case evaluation procedures in a family and children's service agency: integration of practice and research." Journal of Social Service Research 3, 1.

REID, W. J. (1975) "A test of a task-centered approach." Social Work January: 3-9.

––– (1970) "Implications of research for the goals of casework." Smith College Studies in Social Work February: 140-154.

THOMAS, E. J. (1975) "Uses of research methods in interpersonal practice," in N. Polansky, Social Work Research. Chicago: University of Chicago Press.

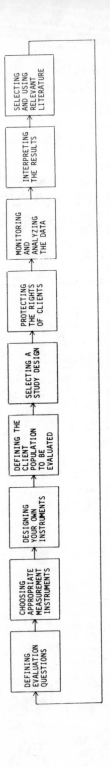

Appendix B

SELECTED PROGRAM EVALUATION PRINCIPLES
AND PRACTICES

This appendix was designed to provide agency personnel with a checklist of selected principles and practices relevant to the program evaluation process. For those who have had prior training in program evaluation techniques, it serves as a refresher. For those without prior training, it serves as a roadmap for the implementation of a program evaluation study and a guide to additional readings. The major principles and practices included in this appendix are listed below.

1. Defining evaluation questions
2. Choosing appropriate measurement instruments
3. Designing your own instruments
4. Defining the client population to be evaluated
5. Selecting a study design
6. Protecting the rights of clients
7. Monitoring and analyzing the data
8. Interpreting results
9. Relevant literature

DEFINING EVALUATION QUESTIONS

How does one select an evaluation question? Although it may be a problem for a group of staff members to formulate one or more questions, individuals working alone may also experience difficulty. To be sure, the question must be of interest to the person or group, and it must be a question for which the answer would be useful. But where do questions come from?

One experienced evaluator sometimes asks the people for whom he is to do an evaluation to write ten answers to the question: "I would like to know

Principle 1	*Why ask a question whose answer would not make a difference anyway?* Do not raise questions about long-range issues when you only have the capacity to utilize answers to short-range questions. Also, remember to make the distinction between a process and an outcome question noted in the previous description of the objectives-oriented model.
Principle 2	*Why ask questions that are inconsistent with your intuitions or beliefs?* For example, if you really do not want to know if paraprofessionals can do an equal or better job of delivering counseling services than professionals, why ask the question? Questions related to unfamiliar, ambiguous, or complex situations are good candidates for program evaluation because staff frequently seek to reduce uncertainty about complex or ambiguous issues by making simplifying assumptions.
Principle 3	*Why ask difficult questions if you are not prepared to deal with the potential conflict frequently caused by the findings?* It is quite common for some aspects of the program evaluation to be flawed (e.g., did not ask enough probing questions or failed to involve a substantial number of clients). Some staff members will discount the findings based on methodological problems. Others may recognize the need to reassess their mode of operations. Program evaluations are likely to generate conflict over ideas that should be viewed as a criterion for a successful evaluation. Similarly, evaluation results may not confirm or clarify previous assumptions and thereby increase uncertainty. If there is no tolerance for such uncertainty, why ask a difficult question?
Principle 4	*Why ask a large question that simply cannot be answered given the realities and constraints of agency life?* Big questions (e.g., "Did our program make our clients get better?") that call for concrete answers are usually not manageable. Small, specific questions are easier to answer with program evaluation methods.

FIGURE B.1   There's Nothing Better Than a Good Question

_____ about my agency." If a group is responding, the individual lists can be consolidated by using small group discussions. The questions selected may or may not explicitly involve agency goals. Questions, however, should be freely selected from among issues that are important to the agency. Given a particular program evaluation question, how does an agency staff decide whether evaluation data will have enough utility to be worth the effort? We suggest the four principles found in Figure B.1.

Although questions can vary substantially in form and content, we suggest that there are three basic types of questions: (1) the descriptive question, (2) the cause-effect question, and (3) the relative effect question. The simplest and most manageable type is the *descriptive question* (e.g., are our clients getting better?). The answer to such questions would normally consist of frequency distributions, means, graphs, and possible tests of significance for the amount of change. Such descriptive questions are excellent beginning points for program evaluations.

The second type of question asks about *absolute causes or effects:* Did a particular treatment program cause the client change noted? Many people who sound as though they are asking the descriptive question, "Is there a change?" are in fact asking this more specific type of question: "Did our treatment cause a change?" It is important to clarify questions of this type to determine the intent behind the language of the question. Unfortunately, this type of question is very difficult to answer because the required experimental conditions are difficult to define and maintain. For this reason, we recommend against asking this type of question for a small evaluation project; limited program evaluation resources are better spent elsewhere.

The third type of question which has greater potential for internal utility asks about *relative effects,* where the comparison may be between programs (e.g., "Is time-limited better than unlimited counseling?") or between groups of clients ("Do middle-class clients benefit more from the program than lower-class clients?"), or may combine both program and client characteristics ("Do clients do better when their counselors are from the same racial/ethnic background?"). Nearly any study designed to answer such questions will require more time and energy than most descriptive studies. At the same time, the potential benefits are correspondingly better. Answers to such questions can be powerful and convincing tools for shaping program and policy development.

CHOOSING APPROPRIATE MEASUREMENT INSTRUMENTS

The choice of measurement techniques involves selection from among a series of instrument characteristics. Different instruments focus on or emphasize different types of outcome variables, including, for example:

Client satisfaction:	How would you rate the quality of the services you received?
Social adjustment:	How well do you get along with the people you spend the most time with?
Symptomatology:	In the past few days, how often have you felt sad or depressed?
Work performance:	How much time from work have you lost in the past 30 days?
School performance:	How would you rate your performance in school?

The choice of instruments should be determined by the user's requirements, which in turn should be based on program objectives. It is advisable to sample a variety of instruments for possible multiple measures. Some instruments require the use of an overall global judgment of status or outcome; others require multiple judgments on different dimensions of behavior. For example, a global scale might ask, "Based on your overall knowledge of the client, rate his/her level of impairment on the following 10-point scale." Global scales are often easier and cheaper to implement.

Evaluating the utilities of instruments also involves assessing their prior use and soundness. Classically the two major measurement ("psychometric") properties of instruments are *reliability* and *validity*. Unfortunately, the importance attached to these is not merely academic. Both reliability and validity are concepts involved in discussing basic patterns, or systematic variation, in the data. If there are no patterns, neither will there be significant results. If you do a study without paying proper attention to reliability and/or validity, you have a good chance of wasting your time and money.

What is "proper attention?" Traditionally there are three types of reliability: internal consistency, interrater reliability, and test-retest reliability. *Internal consistency* is a measure of the degree to which the set of items on a scale tend to measure the same thing. Internal consistency is important any time a set of items or questions are selected and combined to produce a single score on the assumption that each item is measuring part of the same underlying characteristic. In such cases, if internal consistency is not high, the resulting variable will not have coherent meaning and cannot produce systematic results. Internal consistencies are best measured by a statistic called "alpha," which looks and acts like a correlation coefficient (i.e., ideally above .90 and not much below .70).

A second type of reliability is *interrater reliability,* which assesses the agreement among observers in instrument scores or ratings assigned to clients. Obviously this type of reliability is relevant only if other persons, like counselors or significant others, are attributing scores to the client. Interrater reliability is an indicator of the degree to which the scale or set of items means the same thing or is used the same way by different raters. The expected correlation value will usually be lower than the instrument's internal consistency. Interrater reliability may be artificially reduced if the raters are exposed to completely different samples of client behavior. Similar to internal consistency, the reliability should be high, leading to a consistent meaning of the variable, and thereby increase the chances of systematic results.

The third major type of reliability is *test-retest reliability.* This is the correlation between two different administrations of the same instrument, generally when these are separated in time. This correlation is also expected to be smaller than the internal consistency. But in this case, in addition to reductions in reliability due to what we think of as error sources, the correlation may also be reduced if the clients change in varying degrees on the instrument over time and the scores accurately reflect these changes. Thus, a test-retest reliability coefficient is meaningful only if the characteristic being measured is not expected to change during the time interval. For this reason, test-retest reliabilities are of little value for moods, which fluctuate daily, but may be useful for presumably stable characteristics like intelligence.

Proper attention to reliability definitely means an internal consistency reliability calculated on your data set. If your counselors are making ratings, it should also mean interrater reliability checks. If significant others are making ratings, it would be nice to get some test-retest reliabilities, even if only by repeating a few items within the questionnaire. Once established, both internal consistency and test-retest reliability should remain stable, since these are largely inherent characteristics of the instrument. Interrater reliability, on the other hand, is not necessarily stable, and unless it is periodically monitored may decline significantly in the course of study.

With respect to validity, the issues are both simpler and more complex. Validity is defined as the degree to which a score is actually measuring what it is supposed to measure. Often validity is based on circular logic: A new measure of depression is validated if it correlates with old measures of depression and/or if theoretically based predictions or hypotheses about how it will perform prove to be correct. Validity is a difficult concept to deal with satisfactorily.

For purposes of agency program evaluation, the most important form of validity is *face validity.* Face validity is simply the degree to which people accept, at an intuitive level, the judgment that an instrument is measuring what it is supposed to measure. Researchers generally have a rather low opinion of face validity, because they know that intuition can be misleading (e.g., items that "obviously" measure a particular characteristic often do not produce scores that reflect that characteristic). On the other hand, evaluators know that unless the staff really believe that, for example, a measure of depression really is a measure of depression, the data will not be trusted or used. Therefore, face validity is sufficient for agency program evaluation purposes.

Whenever possible, it is advisable to use instruments that have already been developed. These have two advantages: First, someone else did the basic work on getting the items together, providing a systematic set of responses and, it is hoped, investigating the measure's reliability and validity. Second, if you use the scale as designed, you have some reference against which to compare your results.

On the other hand, there is much to be said for starting with someone else's instrument and revising it to make it more suitable for your present purposes. Rarely will you find a measuring technique that accomplishes exactly what you want. If the available instruments are not sufficiently satisfactory, change them. For example, suppose you wanted measures on three different scales: mental status (primarily anxiety and depression type of content), social adjustment (basically, how well does the client get along with people), and client satisfaction. You might survey available instruments and find that no single one really meets your needs. But you might also find that you liked the Client Satisfaction Questionnaire (Larsen, Attkisson, and Hargreaves, n.d.) for its content, and the Psychological Distress Scale from the Denver Community Mental Health Questionnaire (Ciarlo and Reihman, 1974) for a mental status scale. You might also like some of the social adjustment items on the Denver questionnaire but decide that these need to be supplemented by further items from the Community Adaptation Schedule (Roen and Burnes, 1968) along with a few items you write yourself. When you put all these together, you find they do not fit perfectly. Some of the items are worded differently from others, and they have different numbers of responses and may be scored in different directions. You may need to rewrite the items and the responses so they are consistent. The cost of this is that the results from this new instrument are not comparable to results from the original instruments. The advantage is that it appears to meet your need and therefore has greater face validity.

This practice of borrowing from the work of others is common in the social sciences. Except for copyrighted materials (and even these may be paraphrased or changed to reflect your own ideas), it may be done with complete freedom. The sources of your items or ideas for items should, of course, be acknowledged. If you follow a course such as this, it is recommended that you check at least the internal consistency reliability of your new instruments.

DESIGNING YOUR OWN INSTRUMENTS

When designing a structured interview schedule or mailed questionnaire, keep in mind the respondents' level of education, known biases, interests, and other characteristics that might influence responses. The following discussion highlights important aspects of questionnaire construction (taken from *Survey Savvy,* Massachusetts League of Women Voters, 1979). The following principles are important in the development of instrument questions:

— Remember that each question must elicit a response that gives clear, measurable information. More than one question may be necessary for each idea. Each question should be simply worded, short, and to the point.

— Ask only those questions that serve the purpose of the survey.

- Ask only those questions that call for information which respondents can be expected to know. People often guess if they do not know the answers.

- Ask only those questions that cannot be answered readily by other means.

- Do not ask personal questions such as income, voting preference, or intimate behavior unless necessary.

- Do not ask questions that require research or complex mathematical computation by the respondent.

- Do not use names of persons or institutions that may bias answers.

The collection method determines the maximum number and complexity of questions. A questionnaire that will be filled out by the respondent should not require more than 15 minutes to complete. Face-to-face interviews should be less than half an hour in a home or office setting and less than 5 minutes on the street. A phone interview should be completed in less than 15 minutes.

There are generally two types of questions, open-ended and fixed-choice. *Open-ended questions* can be answered in any form the respondent chooses—from a phrase to a paragraph. They are useful in exploratory probing in firs drafts of questionnaires in order to set and identify the range of possible answers. They do not limit the range of responses, but they are often difficult to analyze. *Fixed-choice questions* are answered by checking an appropriate reply and are easy to tabulate. They are useful when you know enough about the population being interviewed and the issues of interest to ask specific questions, and when you know the range of likely responses. All possible choices must be available. For instance, age categories could be "under 21," "21-29," "30-44," "45-65," and "over 65," so there is a category for each respondent and no one could fall into more than one group. In addition, for those who do not know their age or do not choose to divulge it, include categories such as "no opinion," "don't know," or "not applicable" so that the available answers are both inclusive and exclusive.

Rating scales are used to measure attitudes or behaviors. Respondents answer such questions by indicating with the use of a visual aid the degree of opinion, marking a position on a line scaled from, for example, "Strongly agree" to "strongly disagree." Points on a rating scale generally do not exceed four or five units. Opinions vary as to whether there should be a midpoint at which a respondent can indicate "no strong feeling" or "no opinion." Each point on the scale should be defined so that the respondents and the agency staff have a common definition of the units.

Filtering questions are used to eliminate respondents whose answers to some of the questions would be irrelevant due to their lack of knowledge or certain personal characteristics. For example, when interviewing people at a train station about service and possible state subsidies for elderly riders, many questions might be appropriately answered by all passengers. Riders from outside the state, however, would not have to pay for a state subsidy, so their answers about such a subsidy would be irrelevant. A filter question, "Do you live in this state?" should precede the questions concerning a state subsidy. The interviewer should be instructed to omit those questions if the response to the filter question was "no."

The *wording* of questions is also important, and the following guidelines are useful:

— Consider the average reading level of the survey group when preparing the introduction and questions. When surveying the general public, remember that 45 percent of Americans who are 25 and older have not completed high school.

— Be sure the words used have the same meaning for everyone. For example, "environment," "rural atmosphere," or "poor" have many different interpretations. Define terms that may be ambiguous to the respondents.

— Include only one idea in each question.

— Design questions to minimize the number of words in questions and answers.

— Ask questions as they appear in other studies if the intent is to compare results.

— Be specific when asking questions about frequency or quantity.

    POOR: "Do you often eat dinner at home?   Yes   No"

    GOOD: "How many days a week do you eat dinner at home each week?   0-3, 4-7, Don't know." Or "Do you eat dinner at home four or more times a week?   Yes   No"

— State questions neutrally. Do not bias questions with a particular point of view.

    POOR: "Most parents believe that teenagers today lack respect for their elders. Do you agree?"

— Do not use double negatives or unfamiliar abbreviations or initials.

— Do not use general terms such as "often," "many," "usually," or "happy."

The sequence in which questions appear can also influence the answers. Generally, open-ended questions precede closed-ended ones, and general questions precede specific ones. The questions most important for the survey should come first. But less sensitive queries should precede more difficult ones in order to relax the respondent. Questions should occur in a logical order so there are no surprises for the respondent.

The layout of a questionnaire should be clear and attractive. Questions and answers should be arranged logically so that significant data are readily apparent with plenty of space for answers and comments. If the layout is arranged so that all answers are in a column that is separate from the questions, it will be easier to tabulate the answers. The questionnaire should be dated, with pages numbered, and include special notes, such as (OVER) or (CONTINUED ON PAGE __) if questions are continued on another page.

Questionnaires and interview schedules should be pretested to "work the bugs out." In fact, several pretests may be required. The first pretest can involve a few informally selected people, since major problems will probably surface right away. At least one pretest should include a sample similar to that for the actual survey. Analysis of responses will uncover ambiguous or unnecessary questions, threatening or condescending wording, and unclear instructions. If you are pretesting open-ended questions to find a good variety of answers to use with the questions as closed-ended questions in the final draft, you may need to interview 50 people to be sure you have included all the most likely responses. Be sure no one in the pretest will be part of the final sample.

In addition, pretesting can indicate a preferred format or distribution and collection strategy. Test only one variation at a time: either alternative drafts of a cover letter or methods of distribution and collection. Six to eight responses provide enough feedback for each format.

Pretest respondents should receive, complete, and return the questionnaires, and their responses should be analyzed, in the same manner as the process planned for the total sample. In order to learn more about how pretest respondents react to the questionnaire, these people should also be asked some special questions about the tone, clarity, and organization of the questionnaire. For in-depth reactions, separate telephone or personal interviews may be needed.

The preparation of interviewers involves training them to secure respondents' permission for the interview, establish rapport quickly, obtain unbiased information, and record it accurately for quoting, tabulation and analysis. A good interviewer should grasp the objectives of the study, understand the importance of accuracy and consistency, and be committed to the project. This is *not* to say that professional interviewers are necessary for community surveys. It is perfectly feasible to use staff, clients, or community volunteers. A number of youth-serving agencies have recruited and used community youths to conduct community surveys. If sensitive information is collected, it is important that interviewers not be acquainted with the people they interview to avoid bias, embarrassment, and violations of confidentiality.

For most of the training sessions, the trainees should practice interviewing in sections of not more than 15 trainees. Role-playing, with trainees assuming the role of the respondents, is an effective teaching technique. The trainer can also play the part of the respondent and set up problems interviewers may confront. Interviewers should practice listening attentively. During the role-playing session, observers practice recording responses and then compare their answers with the rest of the group.

Training becomes more valuable when reinforced by individual consultation after actual interviewing begins. The trainer should review the first few completed questionnaires with the interviewer or attend the initial interview to provide immediate assistance. In an extensive survey, if time permits, the group of interviewers should be called together again after each has completed some interviews to share experiences, infuse new enthusiasm, and rekindle confidence.

DEFINING THE CLIENT POPULATION TO BE EVALUATED

As with the specification of instrument items, the major clue as to what client population to study should come from the question being investigated in the study. Does it imply or specify one or more particular client groups? If so, then these obviously are to be targeted. If not, client selection is an open issue.

The basic question about defining the population is generalizability, "To what group of clients (or to what class of programs) do you want your results to extend or to be applicable?" For either clients or programs this target for generalization should be defined in advance of data collection, because unless all available subjects and treatments are to be included as subjects, the only way to assure generalizability is to select randomly from among the entire eligible population of clients and treatments the sample from whom data will be collected. No ethical issue is raised here, since there is no suggestion of withholding treatment or offering different treatments. The simple issue is, if you cannot collect data from everyone, the sample should be randomly chosen.

In practice, random selection can be hard to implement. In addition, the random sample you start with may become nonrandom due to subjects providing incomplete data for various reasons (subject "attrition"). When this occurs, two types of steps are taken: First, on whatever variables are available (often age, sex, race, and initial severity of problem) the clients who complete the study are compared with the ones who drop out, as well as with the general population, to determine whether differences can be identified.

Second, since the results cannot be applied with complete assurance to the population, this fact should be acknowledged and conclusions qualified appropriately.

Recognizing the many difficulties, random selection may be approached as follows: First, define the characteristics of the population (e.g., all clients who will be served by a particular clinic in the next six months who volunteer to participate, or all male clients served last year between the ages of 12 and 18 whose primary presenting problem was drug abuse). Second, either list all the eligible persons (for retrospective studies) or decide how all the eligible persons will be identified as they appear (for prospective studies). Third, pick names from the list in such a way that everyone has an equal chance of being selected.

The easiest way to actually sample is as follows: You must know how many names are or will be on the list. Divide this number by the number to be in the sample, and round off this value. For example, if your list included 950 names, and your desired sample size was to be 75, then 950 divided by 75 equals 12.67. This ratio could be rounded off to 12, which would give an expected sample size of 79 (12 divided into 950), or 13 for an expected size of 73 (13 divided into 950). In general, it is better to underestimate the size of the list and round the ratio downward, since both these moves will tend to lead to too large a sample (an easier problem to manage than too small a sample).

Once the ratio is determined, in our case 12, then from among the first 12 names (or whatever ratio is to be used) one is randomly chosen. This may be accomplished by flipping a coin, using a table of random numbers in a statistical text, or actually writing each integer 1 through 12 on a piece of paper and drawing one from a sack. If the number 7 was chosen by one of these techniques, then the seventh name on the list would become the first subject.

Subsequent subjects are selected by taking every twelfth name (e.g., numbers 7, 19, 31, etc.) or by repeating the random selection for each set of 12. If we wanted to select a sample of 250 from a list of 600 names, our ratio would be rounded off to two. We would randomly select one of the first two names (flip a coin: heads is 1, tails is 2), and then every second name from then on.

If no list can be made, as might occur if sampling were to be done from among new admissions, sampling can be done as the list develops, in ways analogous to the procedures already described. For example, if an agency expected 30 new admissions per month and wanted to sample 15, then they could select every second client who is admitted for the study, or for each two admissions in sequence, randomly select one. If different groups are to be sampled (e.g., males and females), then separate lists could be kept for each group. When two men (or women) are admitted, one would be selected as above.

Most people have an intuitive understanding that small samples lead to unreliable results (i.e., results which may be substantially higher or lower than actual population values). This is true because smaller samples may not sufficiently average out potential extreme scores. Because of this unreliability, small samples are also less likely to detect group differences when such differences actually exist. Sample sizes may be chosen on the basis of the size necessary to detect certain differences. Generally sample sizes are selected on the pragmatic basis of resource constraints (e.g., time, money, or subject pool).

Most agencies will probably adopt the pragmatic approach in defining sample size. However, if samples are too small (e.g., under 10 or 15), the likelihood of statistically significant results becomes quite small. For this reason, as a very rough rule of thumb, no group for which important comparisons are to be made should be smaller than 30. An excellent reference for determining statistical power is Cohen (1977).

SELECTING A STUDY DESIGN

The term "study design" refers to the particular way in which subjects are divided into groups and the pattern in which the groups receive the "experimental conditions." The term "treatment" is often used in the literature to encompass any and all variations in group conditions. Any change in outcome, such as an improvement in client functioning, can be the result of factors other than (or in addition to) the counseling the client received. A family, work, or school problem might improve with time. Therefore, other factors may exist as alternative explanations for service outcome.

The purpose of the experimental design is to reduce, or ideally to eliminate, these alternatives, so that when an effect is found it can be attributed unequivocably to the treatment being studied. An ideal design allows comparison of the treated group with other groups which differ from the treatment group only in terms of the treatment itself, not with respect to history, experience, maturation, stress, or expectation.

Rigorous designs are those capable of eliminating many alternative explanations. Against this major advantage are the disadvantages of rigorous designs: They generally require random assignment of subjects to conditions, they tend to be technical in nature and require careful monitoring and prompt response to deviations from plans, once started they are not flexible, and they still rarely (if ever) provide unequivocal answers. By contrast, nonexperimental and quasi-experimental designs are simpler in all respects to implement but far more difficult to analyze and interpret. The evaluator has a choice: trouble at the front end with difficult implementation but with results that are easy to interpret, or easy implementation with trouble in the analysis and interpretation. The following discussion includes two basic designs—the single group pre-post and the multiple group.

Single group, pre-post design. This is probably the most common design used in evaluations. It consists of a single group of subjects who receive a single type of treatment and are tested twice, once before and once after the treatment. This design can be diagrammed as follows:

(premeasure)----(treatment)----(postmeasure)

An example would occur if a group of clients who were about to enter a group therapy program were administered a measurement of anxiety before the group sessions begin, and again six weeks later, for the purpose of comparing anxiety levels at the two times. Similarly, in an ongoing group, clients might be given the measure as they enter and again six weeks later, each on his or her own schedule.

This evaluation design is descriptive and nonexperimental. This means that it can tell you whether a change occurs in client levels on the measures used, but if there is change, it cannot explain why the change occurred. The group average might improve, for example, because of treatment, but it might also improve because of passing time, improved work conditions, or changes in diet. Because only one group and two measurements are involved, it is not possible to separate out the different factors.

Nonetheless, this is an acceptable design to use, especially as a first program evaluation project. It is an easy, cheap design to implement and one that is likely to fit into existing procedures. The data are often interesting and useful, and usually favorable. The major problem with the design will be a tendency to overinterpret: Favorable changes cannot be attributed to the treatment program alone, and the lack of favorable change cannot be explained by presuming that the program is ineffective.

Multiple group designs. All experimental and most quasi-experimental designs involve multiple subject and/or multiple treatment groups. These designs are indicated anytime the outcome question implies that different types of clients will respond differently to a program ("This treatment program will help men more than women"), or that different programs will have differential general effects ("Our socialization program will do a better job of reducing isolation than individual counseling"), or an interaction between the two ("Elderly clients will show more improvement if the program includes a component which enhances a feeling of autonomy").

Naturally there are many variations in these designs. Simple designs involve only one kind of distinction among groups, based either on client characteristics or treatment characteristics. For example:

A. Group 1:   Male clients
    Group 2:   Female clients

B. Group 1:   Clients served in their homes
    Group 2:   Clients who come to the agency for services

C. Group 1:   Clients with drug problems only
    Group 2:   Clients with drug and mental health problems

These designs may involve more than two groups, but increasing the number of groups makes it more difficult to manage the study. Three or four groups should be considered a maximum (e.g., clients from three or four geographical areas or three or four ethnic groups, clients with three or four kinds of presenting problems).

It may be that clients will be classified in two ways. These might be two different client characteristics, two different program characteristics, or one of each. For example:

Group 1A: Black female clients
Group 1B: White female clients
Group 2A: Black male clients
Group 2B: White male clients

Group 1A: Individual therapy with medication
Group 1B: Individual therapy without medication
Group 2A: Group therapy with medication
Group 2B: Group therapy without medication

Group 1A: Black clients seeing Black staff
Group 1B: Black clients seeing White staff
Group 2A: White clients seeing Black staff
Group 2B: White clients seeing White staff

Such designs are quite complex, and more than two distinctions along each factor may become unmanageable.

How do you select a design? In referring back to your question, does it imply distinctions among types of clients, or between types of treatment, or both? Along what dimensions are the distinctions to be made? How many distinctions are implied? If no distinctions are required, you are probably asking a simple descriptive question, or it may be that you have too many distinctions and will need to simplify your question. In any case, *the design is implicit in the question.*

Assignment of clients to treatment conditions, however, may be done either randomly or nonrandomly. Random assignment is preferred because it is the best way to obtain groups that are comparable initially. Then if posttreatment group differences are found, they can be attributed to the treatment with relative confidence. The use of random assignment vastly simplifies the process of data analysis and interpretation.

PROTECTING THE RIGHTS OF CLIENTS

Program evaluation has two primary ethical requirements: first, to protect the human rights of the client-subjects, and second, to never interfere in the legitimate delivery of appropriate services. If the clients are put "at risk" in any way during the program evaluation process, then informed consent should be obtained, preferably in writing, prior to the inclusion in the study and prior to any randomization. "Risk" includes any type of psychological risk and should be broadly interpreted, certainly to include any risk of loss of confidentiality or violation of privacy. Informed consent should probably be acquired if data are to be collected solely for the purpose of evaluation, and especially if data are not collected from all clients. The informed consent form should (1) explain the purposes of the study, (2) explain the risks and benefits of the study to the client, (3) urge the client to ask questions for clarification, (4) explicitly assure that cooperation is voluntary, may be partial and may be withdrawn at any time, and (5) assure that if cooperation is withheld or withdrawn, the provision of services will in no way be affected.

The client and the evaluator should sign a copy of the form and the client should be given a copy to keep, on which should be the investigator's name, address, and phone number. Figure B.2 illustrates such a form. In some larger organizations there are formal review groups which must approve projects, including informed consent procedures, before they may be implemented.

Procedural arrangements must be explicit. For example, probably the first procedure for each client involved in the evaluation will be obtaining informed consent. This information may be presented to the client by a secretary, records clerk, or counselor. It may be the same person for all clients (e.g., a receptionist) or different people for each client (e.g., the client's counselor). Whatever way is selected, the persons involved must be aware of their responsibility, must be instructed in how to fulfill it, and must be monitored to assure that they do fulfill it.

If selection is to occur, then the eligible clients who do consent to participate represent the subject pool. The person planning the study must specify who will keep this list, by what means she or he will be sure of listing every appropriate client, and what process will be followed to select names from the list.

To the Client:

In order to learn more about the effectiveness of our treatment program, we would like to ask you some questions about how you have been doing. If you agree to help us, we will ask you questions about:

1. How you are feeling.
2. Whether the services helped you and, if so, how much.
3. How you are getting along with family and friends.
4. How your work is going.
5. Whether you're having any trouble with alcohol or drugs.
6. Whether you've had any recent trouble with the law.

You should also know that:

7. The information you give will be kept private and confidential. It will not be given to anyone else, not even your counselor or members of your family, unless you want someone else to have it.
8. Participation in this interview is completely voluntary. If you agree to be interviewed but don't want to answer certain questions, that's okay. You can also quit at any time if you change your mind.
9. If you do not agree to be interviewed, or if you don't want to answer certain questions, or if you want to quit later, it will not affect the services you receive now or later, or be held against you in any way.
10. If you have any questions, you are encouraged to call me collect at (206) xxx-xxxx. You may do so prior to your decision to participate.

Thank you for your help.

Sincerely,

Gary Cox, Ph.D.
Project Supervisor

I have read or listened to the above information about the interview.

I understand any answers I give will be confidential and that my participation is completely voluntary.

I have been asked if I have any questions and, if I have, they have been answered. I have been given a signed copy of this consent form, and I understand that if I have any questions I can contact either the interviewer or the project supervisor.

I agree to do the interview.

Client's Name _____
                          (Print)

Client's Signature _____   Date _____

Interviewer's Name _____
                              (Print)

Interviewer's Signature _____

FIGURE B.2   Sample Interview Consent Form

MONITORING AND ANALYZING THE DATA

Evaluation projects tend to wander from their projected courses. This may result from many causes, including staff indifference or even resistance, inexperience with the requirements of program evaluation, lack of clear purposes, changes in purposes, or insufficient time or resources. Loss of quality is likely to take the form of either incomplete or inaccurate data or an insufficient number of subjects. For this reason, probably the two most useful characteristics of the study to monitor in order to detect deterioration are, first, the number of potential and actual subjects and, second, the thoroughness with which data are provided.

Forms should be developed to monitor client attrition and should be used in client follow-up after treatment or discharge. Such forms should indicate the number of subjects who are supposed to be seen, the number lost to the study for each reason, the number interviewed, and the number carried forward to the next week. These numbers can be followed from week to week to detect any undesirable trends. If a particular source of attrition is (or becomes) too great, steps could be taken to correct it. If different inter-viewers are involved, they might be compared to determine if one needed special help.

Similarly, questionnaires or interview schedules should be checked to en-sure that they are legible and complete and that the data values are accurate or at least plausible. Since most data problems are usually due to missing or carelessly supplied information, this check will probably be sufficient. Wher-ever possible, interrater or test-rater reliabilities are highly desirable additional checks for data quality.

Organizing the data. Keypunched cards are the common tools for getting data into a computer. If the size of the data set does not warrant keypunch-ing, the data can be hand-tabulated.

Data may be keypunched directly from the evaluation instruments if they have been precoded, or they may first be transcribed onto "code sheets." The former is preferable. It not only reduces the likelihood of transcription errors (almost impossible to detect) but is faster and therefore cheaper. It does require more careful preparation of forms, since these must be designed to minimize keypunch problems, but this advanced planning is desirable. On a well-prepared instrument, column numbers will accompany each variable, and the card and subject identification number (ID) will be apparent as well as noted in Figure B.3.

Every punched card should include complete ID information: Subject ID, data type (possibly a form number), and/or a card number. If there is any chance that a given person may be included more than once in the study, the ID information for every subject should include a date or admission number. Each of these should occur in exactly the same columns on every card.

HOSPITAL PREREGISTRATION DATA COLLECTION SHEET

Card column

A. CARD #1   (1)

B. FORM #20   (2-3)

C. SUBJECT #   / / / / /0/ /   (4-9)

D. DATE: / / / / / / /   (10-15)

E. D.O.B.:   / / / / / / /   (16-21)

F. AGE: / / / /   (22-24)

G. SEX: F = 1   M = 2   (25)

H. PATIENT'S MARITAL STATUS: (26)

    1 Married   2 Widowed   3 Divorced   4 Separated   5 Single

I. PATIENT'S RELIGION: (27)

    1 Catholic   2 Protestant   3 Jewish   4 Other

J. PATIENT'S SOCIAL SECURITY NO.:   (28-36)

    / / / / – / / / – / / / /

K. PATIENT'S ZIP CODE: (37-41)

    / / / / / /

L. FAMILY MEMBER'S ZIP CODE: (42-46)

    / / / / / /

M. PATIENT HAS MEDICARE?   (47)

    Y = 1   N = 2

N. PUBLIC ASSISTANCE?   (48)

    Y = 1   N = 2

O. ADDITIONAL HEALTH INSURANCE COVERAGE?

    Y = 1   N = 2   (49)

_____(50-52)

(staff signature)

_____

(staff code number)

SOURCE: From the Geriatric and Family Services Clinic, University Hospital,
    University of Washington

FIGURE B.3   **Keypunch Form**

Choice of columns is completely arbitrary but must be consistent. This principle is based on the assumption that if the cards are dropped or shuffled, information will be available in the same place on every card in order to permit reconstituting the deck of cards.

One major reason for analyzing data is to *summarize and/or detect patterns* in the numbers. Simple, self-evident or easily explained analyses are best for evaluation projects, involving descriptive or graphic methods such as frequency distributions, scattergrams, and cross-tabulations (see Figure B.4).

A second major reason for doing data analyses is to *put the results* (i.e., the patterns in the data) *into a context* or frame of reference. The results need to be compared against some standard. Many standards are possible, including program goals, professional norms, or agency or public expectations. An experimental study design will be used in the following discussion to illustrate the data analysis process. Since data analysis frequently refers to graphic or numerical summaries and interpretations, nearly any data set can be analyzed. Data that are routinely collected can be dealt with using simple graphs. Special purpose projects will usually involve more intensive analyses, although even here graphics (histograms, scattergrams) are a good beginning.

Statistical tests are one way to put results into a context, but it is a context of a very particular type. For one thing, the term "statistical significance" simply means that the pattern of results found (such as a difference between two group averages, or a level of correlation between two variables) is large or strong enough that it is unlikely to have occurred by chance. In other words, a statistically significant result is extreme enough that it probably results from some "real" group difference (or relationship or whatever), so a repeat of the study should show the same pattern of results. A nonsignificant result, on the other hand, could occur by chance; a second test might be less strong or even reversed. In this sense, statistical significance is an indicator of the stability of a pattern or result.

But statistical significance does not automatically mean social or practical significance. With large samples, very small or even trivial effects can become statistically significant. The soundest course here is to say that if a result is statistically significant, then it is reasonable to proceed to the next step to see whether or not it is programmatically significant. If a result is nonsignificant, it has no real, reliable statistical meaning. The latter part of this rule can be violated in at least two ways: Staff may act to correct a negative pattern of results even though it is not statistically reliable. For example, a scattergram of service volume may show a two-month downward trend, and the staff may take steps to correct this even though the pattern is not statistically significant.

The second use of unreliable results may occur when a positive nonsignificant result is found and the agency chooses to make public use of the analysis. Depending on the level of candor and openness about the quality of

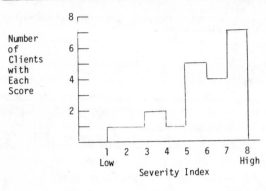

FREQUENCY DISTRIBUTION: Describes a distribution of scores for a group of subjects on one variable.

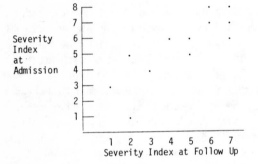

SCATTERGRAM: Shows the joint distribution of two variables. Each point represents the pair of scores for one subject.

	Treatment Plan	
	A	B
Improved	10	8
No Change	6	8
Worsened	3	5

CROSS-TABULATION: Shows the relationship between two variables which have a small number of values. Each entry in the table is the number of subjects with that combination of characteristics (e.g., ten subjects receiving Plan A improved).

FIGURE B.4   Frequency Distribution, Scattergram, Cross-Tabulation analysis, such use may range from completely legitimate to thoroughly dishonest.

Another characteristic of "statistically significant" further complicates these judgments: "Statistically significant" means that there probably is a reliable group difference (or correlation), but it gives no clue whatsoever as to *why* there is a difference. The difference may result from the program, but it may also come from many other sources (preexisting group differences, ordinary changes over time, etc.). As noted in Chapter 7, it is the function of the study design to eliminate such alternatives. If the design is weak, then the meaning of the significant result will remain unclear. Further, an inappropriate statistical analysis may be used, leading to the incorrect appearance of significant differences.

For all of these reasons, we recommend keeping studies simple, focusing on internally directed studies and uses of data, and making modest claims for results when reported externally, including an optional detailed description of the study design and data analyses. Also, we recommend random assignment to groups whenever possible in order to simplify data analysis and interpretation.

Actual choice of the statistical test to be used is determined by the question being asked. The best way to assure relevant analyses is to produce preliminary results and give these to the data users. This should identify misdirected analyses and is likely to lead to refinements and extensions of the analysis.

It is important that results given to the board be thoroughly digested and interpreted by the staff and should include a set of implications and recommendations. Boards of directors are not likely to dig through large volumes of data by themselves. This, in turn, means that the staff is in the best position to do this task, since they are thoroughly familiar with the issues and needs of the organization.

Simple data analyses in small to medium program evaluation projects could be done by hand, often more cheaply and quickly than the computer. Most agencies, however, could utilize computers which are becoming increasingly available, easy to use, and highly cost-effective. The major difficulties of finding a machine and hiring or training a person to analyze the data can be met by contracting with the nearest college or university computer center facility and/or to schools or departments of social work, psychology, or sociology. If you choose to train a person in your own organization, most large computer facilities with statistical software packages (e.g., Statistical Package of the Social Sciences) have training sessions for beginners and ongoing consulting services, usually at minimal cost. Alternatively, students with some computer experience can generally be hired at reasonable hourly rates. A small project (50-100 subjects, with up to 30 variables and no elaborate analyses) could probably be analyzed exhaustively for under $100 in computer time and less than 30 hours of experienced research assistant time. For the same number of subjects, an adequate manual analysis of about five variables could easily take 10-15 hours (assuming some prior knowledge and comfort with statistics). Ten or more variables are essentially beyond the scope of any convenient manual analysis.

The first step of an analysis should be to check that the correct number of cards are present for each subject set and in the correct sequence, and that the subject number is the same on each card within each subject set. Whether the analysis is by computer or hand, the next step should be to graph frequency distributions and scattergrams or cross-tabulations for important pairs of variables. Manual analyses will be limited in the number of cross-tabulations possible.

The functions of this analysis are partly to gain familiarity with the data, to check for data errors, and to check for distributions or relationships between variables which would reduce the validity of statistical tests. If distributions and relationships are acceptable, further analyses, such as single-group pre-post tests, may be made.

The *single-group, pre-post* design is best suited for simple descriptive statistics (means, standard deviations, histograms, scattergrams). Tests of significance (e.g., t-tests) are possible, but the design does not permit determination of the reason for any possible significant group difference. If the single group is to be split into multiple groups (e.g., on sex, age, race), then ideally this should be planned in advance.

For multigroup designs, the choice of analysis depends on how subjects were assigned to groups. Random assignment studies with no significant attrition of subjects may use t-tests or analysis of variance straightforwardly. If a pretest is available, paired t-tests or analysis of covariance should be acceptable and would be more likely to be significant. The groups should be compared on any preintervention measures available, and if dropouts occurred in any number, they should be compared with nondropouts.

Nonrandom assignment complicates the analysis. Nonrandomness occurs with the use of any self-selected and naturally occurring group, and may result from an initially random selection process if there is systematic dropout. The first test is to compare the groups on any available pretest measures, using descriptive techniques and simple t-tests or analyses of variance. Similarly, the correlations between pre- and postmeasure variables can be calculated. Ideally, the magnitudes and patterns of all these will be similar for the different groups. If so, the grounds for comparing the two groups will have been strengthened; if not, they are weakened. Do not, in any case, use "matching" to select similar subjects for the two samples. Also, do not use either t-tests or analysis of variance if the groups are different at pretest. For statistically inexperienced evaluators, or for those with limited resources, statistical consultation is highly recommended.

INTERPRETING RESULTS

Negative results suggest that clients are not improving or are even getting worse. Negative results are not likely to occur with simple pre-post designs, because such studies usually have regression effects built into them. That is, most human problems have ups and downs, and clients are most likely to enter programs, and be given a premeasure, when problems are most severe. Postmeasures are likely to look better because, quite apart from any treatment effects, people with severe problems usually get better over a period of time. In the absence of a control group, a positive change from pre-post-testing cannot be regarded as indicating that treatment was the *sole* cause for improvement.

Pre-post studies can produce negative results, however, and this is most likely to occur when the group being treated is either especially resistant to improvement (e.g., character disorders) or suffering from a chronic condition (e.g., chronically mentally ill). In such cases, success may be defined as stabilizing a condition or reducing the rate of deterioration, but unless the people reviewing the study understand this, the results may appear to be negative. A control group or treatment norms from other programs may be used to demonstrate the relative improvement.

Negative results are much more likely to occur in multiple designs and, in fact, may be more common than not in such studies. The negative results may be real—that is, the groups may truly not be different—but methodological flaws may also cause negative results. The most likely of these methodological problems are the use of preexisting or other nonrandom groups (men and women, in-patients, and out-patients), lack of attention to reliability and validity issues (e.g., improper training of data collectors), other data quality flaws (e.g., differential dropout rates in the groups), or a failure to measure the outcome variables that are really of interest.

Since nearly all evaluations incorporate a few such problems, it is likely to be difficult to decide whether negative results are real or result from the nature of the evaluation methodology. Sometimes more sophisticated data analyses will help resolve the matter. Often the only definite answer will come from repeating the study with an improved design or procedure.

Whether negative results will have negative effects on a program depends on political factors. It is hoped that negative political effects can be partly avoided by analyzing the data in the context of methodological limitations. Certainly negative results need not be useless, since they do represent information, and especially if study weaknesses can be taken into account, they may be of considerable assistance to staff. Be assured, however, that negative results are quite common, especially in program evaluation studies.

Because the designs and/or the data analyses for most evaluation studies have some flaws and because we typically do not know specifically what the effects of these limitations have on the results, the evaluation results often become equivocal. This situation is likely to continue, especially in small program evaluation efforts, and therefore it is clear that results should be interpreted with modesty. Whether staff is explaining the results to the administrator, or an administrator is using the results as part of a decision-making process or presenting them to a board or the public, the conclusions should be treated as tentative. They should be objective, systematic, and rational and can be among the best available, but they nonetheless incorporate uncertainty and probably error. With increasing experience, the quality will improve, but results will, for practical purposes, never be unequivocal.

This fact should not denigrate the value of the data. After all, most information circulating in agencies is biased, incomplete, or inadequate in and of itself for reaching conclusions. Every staff member collects as much information as possible from as many sources as possible and weighs and integrates it in different ways for different purposes. The value and importance of one piece of information is often compared with the total informational context. Evaluation data may complement or conflict with other sources of information commonly available to staff. In this sense evaluation data have considerable potential for balancing one's current view of a program. It is this balancing phenomenon which we think makes program evaluation a key component in a self-evaluating agency.

The last step in the process takes place when staff use evaluation results in making decisions or plans. We do not think that utilization requires that the decision go in the direction implied by the results, since, among other reasons, the evaluation results are only one among many sources of information on which the decision is based. For effective utilization to occur, the data must be relevant to a decision and staff must be aware of the data and their relevance. It seems perfectly clear that the best way to make this happen is to specify the important question for decision making and then make sure that the program evaluation study remains relevant to the question. In other words, *the basis of utilization is in the selection of the issue to be evaluated and the ongoing interaction between the staff and the board.*

PROGRAM EVALUATION LITERATURE

For agency staff and board members interested in acquiring additional understanding of program evaluation principles and practices, there is a large literature to sample. Possibly the best single introduction to evaluation is Patton (1978), a well-written, interesting book which vigorously pushes a particular point of view. Hargreaves et al. (1977) and Weiss (1972) are also good introductory books. Weiss is a small, well-integrated, well-rounded, academically oriented book. Hargreaves et al. is an edited volume with a comprehensive mix of principles and practice. Attkisson et al. (1978) is the most comprehensive and academically oriented of this group and serves as an excellent textbook and reference. In addition, step-by-step how-to-do-it manuals are becoming quite common, such as these:

> Hagedorn et al. (1976) provide a relatively comprehensive set of techniques following an outline much like Hargreaves et al. (1977). Mental health focus.

> Fitz-Gibbon and Morris (1978) do a similar job, oriented toward education. These two tend to cover quite different ground.

> Fink and Kosecoff (1978) provide a much smaller, fairly content-free book of fairly specific steps to go through in designing and implementing an evaluation.

The best reference on "utilization-focused evaluation" is Patton (1978). Glaser's (1976) review monograph of the utilization literature is more academic and has little obvious applicability.

With regard to instrument selection, Waskow and Parloff (1975) include a thorough examination of mental health related measures and issues in measurement, including specific recommendations. Both Hargreaves et al. (1977) and Hagedorn et al. (1976) describe and reproduce a number of instruments. Chun et al. (1975) and Comrey et al. (1973) provide for broader coverage, but in much less depth.

Cohen (1977) is by far the best resource on the power of statistical tests and provides the easiest means for determining the power of a test. Cochran (1977) is technical but widely used as a text on sampling. Other step-by-step manuals on how to compute statistics include Bruning and Kintz (1968) and Morris and Fitz-Gibbon (1978). Linton and Gallo (1975) appears to be a cross between a statistics text and a statistics cookbook which explains and defines terms and provides assistance in selecting the right test. This is a good book for someone who wants a reasonable combination of practicality, increased understanding, and minimal hassle.

There are at least two journals and two major national organizations which focus on evaluation. The journals are *Evaluation Review,* published by Sage Publications, and *Evaluation and Program Planning,* published by Pergamon Press. The national organizations are the Evaluation Research Society and Evaluation Network.

REFERENCES

ATTKISSON, C. C., W. A. HARGREAVES, M. J. HOROWITZ, and J. E. SORENSEN (1978) Evaluation of Human Service Programs. New York: Academic Press.

BRUNING, J. L. and B. L. KINTZ (1968) Computational Handbook of Statistics. Glenview, IL: Scott, Foresman.

CAMPBELL, D. T. and J. C. STANLEY (1963) Experimental and Quasi-Experimental Designs for Research. Chicago: Rand-McNally.

CHUN, T., S. COBB, and J.R.P. FRENCH (1975) Measures for Psychological Assessment: A Guide to 3,000 Original Sources and Their Applications. Ann Arbor, MI: Survey Research Center.

COCHRAN, W. G. (1977) Sampling Techniques. New York: John Wiley.

COHEN, J. (1977) Statistical Power Analysis for the Behavior Sciences. New York: Academic Press.

COMREY, A. L., T. E. BACKER, and E. M. GLASER (1973) A Source Book for Mental Health Measures. Los Angeles: Human Interaction Research Institute. (10889 Wilshire Blvd., Los Angeles, CA 90024)

COOK, T. D. and D. T. CAMPBELL (1979) Quasi-Experimentation: Design and Analysis Issues for Field Settings. Chicago: Rand-McNally.

FINK, A. and J. KOSECOFF (1978) An Evaluation Primer. Beverly Hills, CA: Sage.

FITZ-GIBBON, C. T. and L. L. MORRIS (1968) How to Calculate Statistics. Beverly Hills, CA: Sage.

GLASER, E. (1976) Putting Knowledge to Use: A Distillation of the Literature Regarding Knowledge Transfer and Change. Los Angeles: Human Interaction Research Institute.

HAGEDORN, H. J., K. J. BECK, S. F. NEUBERT, and S. H. WERLIN (1976) A Working Manual of Simple Program Evaluation Techniques for Community Mental Health Centers. DHEW Publication No. (ADM) (Stock No. 017-024-00539-8). Washington, DC: Government Printing Office.

HARGREAVES, W. A., C. C. ATTKISSON, and J. E. SORENSEN (1977) Resource Materials for Community Mental Health Program Evaluation DHEW Publication No. (ADM) 77-328 (Stock No. 017-024-00554-1). Washington, DC: Government Printing Office.

KIRESUK, T. O. and R. E. SHERMAN (1968) Goal attainment scaling: a general method for evaluating community mental health programs." Community Mental Health Journal 4: 443-453.

LINTON, M. and P. S. GALLO (1975) The Practical Statistician: Simplified Handbook of Statistics. Monterey, CA: Brooks/Cole.

Massachusetts League of Women Voters (1979) Survey Savvy. Boston.

MORRIS, L. L. and C. T. FITZ-GIBBON (1978) Evaluator's Handbook. Beverly Hills, CA: Sage.

PATTON, M. Q. (1978) Utilization-Focused Evaluation. Beverly Hills, CA: Sage.

——— (1975) In Search of Impact: An Analysis of the Utilization of Federal Health Evaluation Research. Minneapolis: University of Minnesota Center for Social Research.

ROTHMAN, J. (1980) Using Research in Organizations. Beverly Hills, CA: Sage.

SIEGEL, S. (1956) Nonparametric Statistics for the Behavioral Sciences. New York: McGraw-Hill.

WASKOW, I. E. and M. B. PARLOFF Psychotherapy Change Measures. NIMH DHEW Publication No. (ADM) 74-120 (Stock No. 017-124-397-2 DHEW). Washington, DC: Government Printing Office.

ABOUT THE AUTHORS

MICHAEL J. AUSTIN is Director of the Center for Social Welfare Research, University of Washington School of Social Work. He directed the project which produced this book. His research and teaching interests include social service and mental health administration, personnel management, and supervisory management. He is the author of *Supervisory Management for the Human Services* (Prentice-Hall, 1981) and co-editor of a forthcoming *Handbook of Mental Health Administration* (Jossey-Bass).

GARY B. COX is Research Associate Professor of Psychology, University of Washington School of Medicine, Department of Psychiatry and Behavioral Sciences. He has an extensive background in mental health program evaluation and has served as consultant to numerous local, state, and national agencies. He has contributed over 20 journal articles in the field of evaluative research. One of his most recent publications is "Involuntary Patient Flow: A Computer Simulation of a Psychiatric Ward," in *Evaluation Review,* 1980.

NAOMI GOTTLIEB is Professor and Associate Dean of the University of Washington School of Social Work and Director of the Project on Women and Mental Health. Her teaching and research interests focus on research methodology and services to women. She has written in the areas of the welfare system and child welfare, and her most recent publication is *Alternative Social Services for Women* (Columbia University Press, 1980).

J. DAVID HAWKINS is Assistant Professor at the University of Washington School of Social Work and Co-Director of the National Center for the Assessment of Delinquent Behavior and Its Prevention, Center for Law and Justice. His teaching and research interests include research methodology, juvenile justice, delinquency prevention, and drug abuse prevention. He is a program evaluation consultant to numerous local, state, and national organizations. His substantial publication record includes the publication entitled "Decision Makers' Judgments: The Influence of Role, Evaluative Criteria, and Information Access," *Evaluation Quarterly,* 1978.

JEAN M. KRUZICH is Assistant Professor, University of Wisconsin–
Milwaukee and served as the project coordinator who field-tested previous
versions of this book while completing her doctoral studies at the University
of Washington School of Social Work. Her teaching and research interests
include social service and mental health administration, criminal justice,
evaluative research, and social policy implementation. She has published
several articles, and her most recent book chapter, entitled "The Mentally Ill
Offender," will appear in the forthcoming *Handbook of Mental Health
Administration* (Jossey-Bass).

RONALD RAUCH is a Certified Public Accountant and Senior Accountant
with Price Waterhouse, Seattle. He has considerable expertise in the not-for-
profit sector as auditor of social service agencies and financial management
consultant. He conducts training workshops for administrators and board
members of social agencies.